— THE —
PIGGYBACK FLIGHT
PILOT'S JOURNEY

Story by:
Cyndi Rojohn

Contributor:
David Rojohn

Fulton Books, Inc.
Meadville, PA

First originally published by Fulton Books 2018

ISBN 978-1-63338-818-5 (Paperback)
ISBN 978-1-63338-819-2 (Digital)

Printed in the United States of America

Special thanks and loving thoughts goes out to Glenn H. Rojohn's mother, Selma E. Rojohn, for keeping and preserving her son's World War II history so that his family could learn the story and share it with others.

This book is dedicated to:

The Piggyback Flight crews, the "Bloody Hundredth" and the 350th Squadron.

The Piggyback Flight families who provided additional information, so we could tell the world the legendary story. We are grateful they have been able to make it possible for them to take the second-generation journey with us.

The 100th Bomb Group Foundation for their support of the Glenn H. Rojohn's legendary, historical journey.

The witnesses of the Piggyback Flight who provided us with valuable information. And the other crews who flew the fateful mission to Hamburg, Germany December 31, 1944.

And finally, a special thanks to Michael P. Faley, 100th Bomb Group Foundation Executive Vice President and Historian. Your patience, wisdom and love for the Piggyback Flight and The Bloody Hundredth are greatly appreciated by all involved in this journey.

Lt. Glenn H. Rojohn

A picture tells a thousand words. Documents provide a wealth of detailed information. Censored letters sent from someone participating in war are written for the reader to read in between the lines.

The Rojohn family decided to write the story of the Piggyback Flight Pilot through the pictures, documents, reports, letters, and mission logs that are part of Glenn H Rojohn's World War II collection.

We urge you to look at the documents, reports, and pictures that are also included within the text and at the end of some of the chapters providing detail that we could not provide in the text.

CHAPTERS

CHAPTER 1

ART IMITATING LIFE

At a 2001 100th Bomb Group Foundation Reunion in Omaha, by chance Tom Mabry sat across from Captain Glenn H. Rojohn during a luncheon. Tom was able to hear all of the veterans talk about the war and what the reunions meant to them. Tom Mabry became one of the few to hear Glenn tell his story about the legendary Piggyback Flight.

Tom Mabry later described that luncheon meeting as "One of the most unassuming men I've ever met. You would never know that he was the pilot of one of the most amazing flights in aviation history."

A Rojohn family friend, John Lambert, was a Huey Helicopter Pilot in the Vietnam War. He told me he could not tell his family about his war experiences. Instead the easiest way for him was to write his memoir. He was more comfortable having his family and friends read about his experience when THEY were ready. Also, he wanted to preserve those war stories for future generations. We understood exactly what he meant.

When HE was ready, Lt. Glenn H. Rojohn told his story to the world. He could not tell that story personally to his children or grandchildren. Instead he left his legacy to them in boxes containing letters, documents, log books, diaries, witness accounts, crew member accounts, prints, pictures, cassette tapes, and memorabilia so his family could research his story for themselves. So, they could write the book he could never write himself. He hoped THEY would preserve this amazing, legendary story forever-- the Piggyback Flight Pilot's Journey.

So much occurred during the time he served as a B-17 Bomber Pilot. He is best known for a mid-air collision between two B-17s over the North Sea on December 31, 1944 on his 22nd mission flying back to Thorpe Abbotts from Hamburg, Germany. That legendary, historical mid-air collision from that day on is known as Pick-a-Back, Piggyback, Piggyback Flight by witnesses, historians, veterans, and authors. Lt. Glenn H. Rojohn not only piloted The Little Skipper on that mission, but also landed his ship and Nine Lives simultaneously.

Everyone who serves their country is a hero, especially those involved in war. There aren't many who can say they were commissioned into the Air Force twice. In a way that is what happened to Captain Glenn H. Rojohn.

In 1995, Gregg Thompson, shown with Glenn's wife Jane, painted his rendition of the Piggyback Flight legendary collision. Rojohn, his Navigator Bob Washington, and witness Ralph Christensen worked with Mr. Thompson as advisors to make sure the position of the two B-17s was accurate.

Gregg Thompson, artist, with Jane Rojohn

On October 24, 2008 The Piggyback Flight painting was commissioned into the Air Force as part of a Service Before Self United States Air Force 2008 Art Presentation. Now, both Glenn and an artist's rendition of the incident on his 22nd mission both are part of the Air Force. Unfortunately, the Piggyback Flight Pilot did not live to be part of that commissioning. Glenn's good friend, Bob Walter, contacted PA Senator Arlen Spector to secure three tickets for that event. Mrs. Jane Rojohn was accompanied by her son Dave and Mr. Walter to the event. Unknown to them, Gregg Thompson also planned on attending. The Rojohn family talked with the artist numerous times on the phone throughout the painting and lithograph process. They were extremely grateful to meet him for the first time and thank him personally for preserving the historical collision.

Now YOU have the opportunity to learn Glenn H. Rojohn's journey that ended with the commission of the Piggyback Flight painting into the Air Force.

CHAPTER 2

HOW THE JOURNEY BEGAN

Glenn H. Rojohn lead a simple life in Greenock, Pennsylvania, southeast of Pittsburgh. He grew up on a farm so he loved playing with farm animals and baseball with his brother Leonard. He never could have imagined landing a plane in his families' homeland would change his life forever.

The son of Selma Emilia Beulshausen Rojohn and Harry David Rojohn attended a one-room school house for the elementary grades, pictured second row far left, learning subjects history, math and spelling. Like many of the Greatest Generation, he walked to high school in McKeesport, PA where he was awarded his diploma in 1941. He had a knack for numbers, so

Glenn at home on the farm

his first job was at Union National Bank in McKeesport. It was a job he thought he would keep forever. In addition to working, he attended Robert Morris University in Pittsburgh for accounting. He found new friends. And he was content with his new life a short distance away from the farm.

But the war was raging in Germany and the Pacific. Glenn decided what was best for him and his country was to leave his job, school, and the simple life to follow his family's tradition of service. He decided to join those who were serving their country.

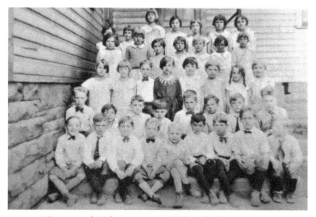

Greenock Elementary School Classmates

CHAPTER 3

TRAINING

Serving their country was something the Rojohn brothers Glenn H. and Leonard E., felt was important to help preserve freedom. They decided to enlist in the Army Air Corp during World War II. Twists of fate placed them in the annals of history.

Necessary letters of recommendation from his pastor, employer, and government officials were written in support of Glenn's commitment to join the war effort. After being sworn in, Glenn left for Company E Barracks 3 at Camp Meade October 24, 1942. He was really looking forward to Cadet training. On October 31, 1942 he was sent back to Pittsburgh because there was not a cadet training class for him to attend.

He didn't want to wait around for a class to begin. So he was assigned to the Pittsburgh recruiting office until a training class was established for him to attend.

While working in the recruiting office he made new friends from all over the Pittsburgh area. One of those friends asked him one day if he would go on a blind date with a "city girl" by the name of Jane McCormick. The

Jane McCormick

"farm boy" wasn't sure how that would work, but he agreed to go on the date. That is when he met the love of his life, shown in her high school graduation picture. Eventually she would become his wife.

Leonard Rojohn decided to leave high School in early April of 1943 to enlist in the Army Air Corp. He was assigned to the Cadet Training class in Nashville, Tennessee. He arrived April 11, 1943. As fate would have it, at the end of March 1943, Glenn Rojohn was reassigned from the recruiting office in Pittsburgh to Cadet Training in Nashville, Tennessee. He arrived in Nashville by train to start his training April 4, 1943. He is pictured with his recruiting class. Glenn is pictured in the top row second from the right.

Glenn's (third on top row) recruiting class

The two brothers were not aware of each others location until Glenn was assigned to KP duty in Leonard's camp not long after arriving for training. A chance sighting reunited the two brothers from the small town of Greenock in Western Pennsylvania. The two Brothers reunited, training together to serve their country. On April 20, 1943 they made history when they were classified for pilot training to train together as bomber pilots.

Before they started Pilot Training, they were scheduled for a short furlough. During that furlough, Glenn told Jane he didn't want to get married because bomber pilot's survival rate was low. Jane loved Teddy Bears so he gave her one to keep her company and remember him until he came back home safe. She kept that bear the rest of her life.

The two brothers continued their training together at Maxwell Field. They arrived May 4, 1943. In Glenn's training diary he described having to endure upperclassmen "treatment" immediately upon arrival. Because Glenn never talked

Jane with gift from Glenn

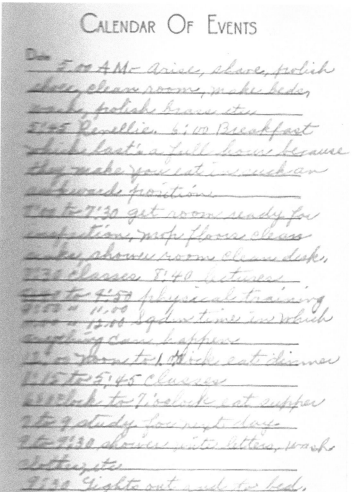

Maxwell Field

about his military experience, it is unknown exactly what that "treatment" was. Glenn kept his Maxwell Field Handbook Pictured in his Army Air Corp Diary is a daily activities entry. He also wrote in his diary "If I had time I could write a book on what happened to me last week but time and upperclassmen won't permit." On May 28, 1943 the Rojohn Brothers became upperclassmen. And on June 3, Glenn and Leonard were assigned to the same squadron, placed in the same barracks to continue their history together. In his training diary, Glenn highlighted his days in the pressure chamber and machine gun shooting.

On July 2, 1943 the two brothers arrived in Vichy, MO. They started to fly July 5. Highlighted in his training diary was his first opportunity to be in a plane – "riding for the first time, handling the controls, and spins." On July 21 he had his first solo flight. On July 24, "I ground looped today and damaged the plane to the extent of $150.00".

From July 29 to August 1, 1943 Glenn and Leonard had a pass so they could have a visit from family. Their parents, their cousin Blanche and Jane McCormick came from the Pittsburgh, PA area to spend time with Glenn and Leonard. Pictured left to right are Blanche Summers, Leonard Rojohn, Selma Rojohn, Glenn Rojohn, Jane McCormick.

A Mother and her son Leonard on left and Glenn on the right. And Leonard, their father Harry Rojohn, and Glenn.

Leonard Mom Glenn   Leonard Dad Glenn

On August 9, 1943, Glenn and Leonard passed their 20 hour check on August 9, 1943 finishing their training at Vichy, MO.

On August 15, 1943 they traveled to Chester Field in McBride MO from Vichy, MO to take their 60-hour check and graduate. The graduation experience included a dance in Perryville with 120 girls and 85 servicemen. Glenn's letters home referred to meeting girls during training, but his heart belongs to the "city girl" from Pittsburgh.

After arriving in Malden, MO on August 31, 1943, they received their real flight suits to train with their class. In Malden they trained in the Basic Trainer. Cross country training was also part of their agenda. Pictured are the two brothers, Leonard the third from the left, Glenn the third from the right, with other cadets.

Malden Field Training Class

Glenn noted that most of the time the two brothers flew the same day on the same flight path with Leonard flying behind him. On October 3rd he documented he talked briefly to Leonard over the radio.

Glenn and Leonard successful completed Basic Training. Shown in their graduation class Glenn is third from right and Leonard is sixth from right.

Leonard and Glenn with Malden buddies

Glenn and Leonard were assigned to Stuttgart, Arkansas for advanced pilot training. They flew together numerous times as part of the training. On November 10 Glenn solved advanced training. December 22, 1943, Glenn passed his instrument check. On January 7, 1944 the two brothers graduated with their class as 2nd Lieutenant. Leonard tenth from the right and Glenn the eleventh, according to the announcement.

Two brothers Glenn and Leonard

THE COMMANDING OFFICER

STUTTGART ARMY AIR FIELD

ANNOUNCES THE GRADUATION OF

CLASS 44-A

ON FRIDAY, JANUARY SEVENTH

NINETEEN HUNDRED FORTY-FOUR

STUTTGART, ARKANSAS

Stuttgart graduating class

After graduation the two brothers left for home to see family and friends as posted in the McKeesport Daily News. On furlough they showed how proud they were of serving their country. Glenn is shown with his mother, Selma. Glenn is shown with their father Harry.

PAGE 26

BROTHER PILOTS of B-17 Flying Fortresses anxious for action, are Lt. Leonard Earl Rojohns, 18, left, and Lt. Glenn Harry Rojohns, 21, of Greenock. Both enlisted as Aviation Cadets here and graduated at the same time at the Stuttgart Army Air Base, Ark. They are the sons of Mrs. Selma Rojohns, of Box 145, Greenock, and are home on furlough.

Home on leave

Glenn with his father

Glenn with his mother

On January 19, 1944, the two Brothers arrived at Chanute Field, Illinois for B-17 transitional training. According to Glenn's notes they had the same instructors and flew together. They flew their first solo together,

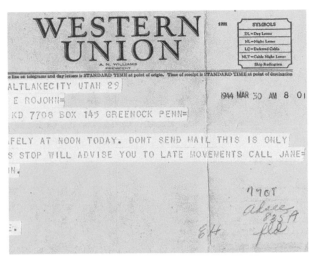

switching seats. In a recorded interview, Glenn mentioned his concern for two brothers training together in the same plane since they were no other children in the family. He asked that they not be in the same plane. That request was granted.

In his training diary, Glenn noted on January 21 "I flew a B-17 for 4 hours."

The brothers picked up their crews in Salt Lake City, UT. According to a telegram sent home. Glenn's crew: Back row left to right – G. W. Hoag 19 from Philadelphia PA., Navigator; B F Jurist from Chicago, Illinois 26 and married, Bombadier; William G. Leek from Everson, Washington, Co-Pilot; Glenn H. Rojohn 22 from Greenock, PA, Pilot; Bottom Row from left to right H. G. Horenkamp from Floressent, Missouri, Tail Gunner; Ed Neuhaus from Toledo, Ohio, Radio

Telegram Arrived in Salt Lake City

Operator; O E Elkin married from Winnsboro, LA, Engineer; Joseph Russo from Chigago, Illinois, Ast. Radio Operator & Gunner; and Roy Little from Cudahy, Wisconsin, Gunner and Ast. Engineer.

Lt Glenn Rojohn's Stateside Crew

Leonard is pictured top left with his crew. Top row Leonard Rojohn, DL Chamberlain, VE Paul, TD Bandar. Bottom Row OK Brantley, RN Schade, C Yevtich, JE Williams, ML Heaherington, JF MacKnyk. They then flew to Dalhart, Texas for overseas training.

In May 4, 1944 they arrived at Gulfport, Mississippi for additional training. During an interview with Terry Flatley for her potential article about the two brothers, Glenn spoke of an experience he had with his crew. It was a forecast of what was to come for the Glenn H. Rojohn crew. The mission on June 23, 1944 took them to Panama City, Florida for a flyover salute for a General. During their flight back, their plane lost one engine and another caught fire. According to Rojohn we lightened the plane. After inspection, the Navigator, George Hoag gave the OK to fly back to Gulfport. Rojohn stated, "It was stressful for all of us."

When he returned from that unnerving flight, Glenn turned on the radio to relax. Or so he thought. On the radio was an emergency broadcast about a tornado that devastated the town of Greenock, PA., his hometown. The real anxiety began. He anguished, "Were his parents still alive? Did he and his brother have a home to go back to?" Days later when the phone lines were restored he was able to contact his parents. The stress was over, only a nicked brick on one of the second-floor corners. The majority of

Greenock tornado damage June 1944

19

his family members were spared from the twister. The worst of the devastation for the Rojohn family was the limbs of the orchard trees that lined the clay tennis court entwined so badly that they never bore fruit again. God was with the Rojohn family on that fateful day. Others were not so lucky. Just feet from the Rojohn home their neighbor's homes were destroyed.

Langley Field, Virginia for radar training was their last training stop.

Training was over. Now it was time for assignment orders to the Pacific or Europe. They didn't have to wait long for an answer. Both Glenn H. Rojohn and Leonard E. Rojohn crews were ready to begin their journey.

The war in the European Theatre was their destiny. It was time to put their training to use. The two brothers were scheduled to fly to Germany in the same group. Unfortunately, Leonard woke up ill with tonsillitis and was unable to fly. Glenn began his solo missions without his brother close by.

The Rojohn brother's entry in World War II history of training together ended when they left Virginia, but another entry in the history books was yet to take place for Glenn.

Documents in Chapter 3

1. Letter of reference for enlistment
2. Training Certification
3. Enlistment Record from Training Diary
4. Front cover of Malden Yearbook
5. Training Certification
6. Flying Regulation Exam
7. Abandon Aircraft Procedure
8. B-17 F Questionnaire
9. Instrument Certification
10. Army Qualification Separation Record
11. Letter 5/25/44 Sent his crew members addresses to his mother

St. Mark's Ev. Lutheran Church
Homestead, Pa.

Peace Lutheran Church
Greenock, Pa.

AUG. J. ENGELBRECHT, PASTOR
224 EAST NINTH AVENUE
HOMESTEAD, PENNA.
HOMESTEAD 1745

⟶)(⟵

September 23, 1942

Commanding General

Third Service Command

Baltimore, Maryland.

Sir:-

Glenn H. Rojohn is a member in good standing of Peace Lutheran Church, Greenock, Pennsylvania. I have known him since I assumed that pastorate in June, 1941. During that time I have come to know him better than might be expected of the usual pastoral relationship. I can describe him as alert, willing, faithful, and unfailingly courteous. His habits are good. His home environment is favorable. He is able to take suggestion. Relationship with superiors, friends and acquaintances is excellent. I feel that I can give him unqualified character recommendation and expect him to be a credit to the arm of the service to which he might belong.

Sincerely,

aug. J. Engelbrecht

Recommendation Letter for enlistment

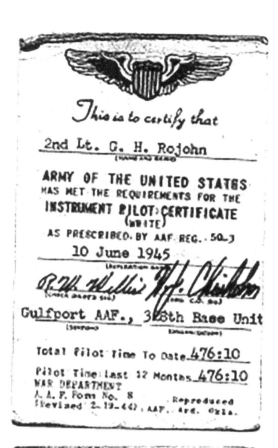

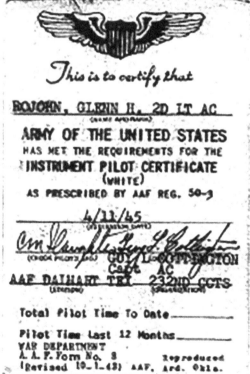

Notice of Pilot Training certification

ENLISTMENT RECORD

Date entered into service *Oct. 24, 1942*

Place *Pittsburgh.*

Registration Number *12052*

Branch of service *Army Air Corp*

Where sent after induction *Camp Meade*

To what outfit assigned *Company 6*
Barracks 3.

COMPANY, REGIMENT, DIVISION OR CORRESPONDING UNIT
IN OTHER BRANCHES

Nature of service *Work in recruiting of*

Rank *Private* serial number *131-*

Other Information

Returned from Camp Meade
Oct 31 - 1942.
Started Position in security
office in old Post office building
Nov 2 - 1942 -
Sent to Nashville Tenn. 4-4-43

Enlistment Record

Maxwell Field Yearbook Cover (entire booklet in collection)

NOTICE OF CLASSIFICATION

Registrant ___Glenn H. Rojohn___ Order No. __12052__

has been classified in Class __I-A__ (Until _____, 19___)
(Insert Date for Class II-A and II-B only)

by ☒ Local Board
☐ Board of Appeal (by vote of _____ to _____)
☐ President

__9-25-42__, 19___   [signature]
(Date of mailing)   Member of Local Board.

NOTICE OF RIGHT TO APPEAL

Appeal from classification by local board or board of appeal must be made by placing appeal form on back of questionnaire at office of local board, or by filing written notice of appeal, within ten days after the mailing of this notice. Before appeal, a registrant may file a written request for appointment, which the must board properly and, if so done so, the local board will fix the and will notify him to appear personally before the local board; if this is done, the registrant is entitled to not fixed beyond the day set by the local board for each appearance.

There is a right in certain dependency cases, of appeal from appeal board decision to the President; see Selective Service Regulations.

The law requires you—To keep in touch with your local board. To notify it of any change of address. To notify it of any fact which might change classification.

D. S. S. Form 57 (Rev. 4-12-41)   16—24073-1   U. S. Government Printing Office

---

NOTICE TO REGISTRANT
TO APPEAR FOR
PHYSICAL EXAMINATION   __Sept. 18, 1942__, 19___
                                        (Date of mailing)

You are directed to report for physical examination by the local board examiner at the time and place designated below:

___Dr. Rowland, Elizabeth, Pa.___
(Place of examination)

at __7:30 P.__ m., on __Sept. 23, 1942__, 19___

This examination will be of a preliminary nature, for the purpose of disclosing only obvious physical defects, and will not finally determine your acceptance or rejection by the armed forces.

If you are so far from your local board area that reporting for the above physical examination will constitute a hardship, you may submit a request to your local board for reference to another local board for preliminary physical examination. Your request must include the following information:
1. The reasons for your request for reference to another local board.
2. The designation (name and location) of the local board having jurisdiction over the area in which you are now located.

Failure to comply with this notice will result in your being declared a delinquent and subjected to the penalties provided by law.

D. S. S. Form 201
(Rev. 4-1-41)   GPO   16—26425-2   [signature]
                                        Member-Clerk of Local Board.

Training Certification for entry into service

FLYING REGULATIONS EXAMINATION

1. Under normal conditions airplanes will be equipped with: How many landing lights?

2. What is the policy regarding the wearing of parachutes in Military Aircraft? What are the exceptions to this?

3. What is the policy regarding landing at airports under construction?

4. What must a pilot do at the termination of his flight if he encounters unusual electrical Phenomena while on a flight?

5. What are airspace reservations?

6. What are the rules governing the right of way of aircraft?

      a. Two approaching head on?
      b. Crossing?
      c. Overtaking?
      d. Landing?

7. What are the normal C. A. A. weather minimum?

8. What are the normal C. A. A. altitude minimum while in flights?

9. How are airways designated? What altitudes are used on these airways?

10. What is the policy regarding passengers riding in military aircraft?

11. How are destructions marked on airports? How are closed runways marked?

      a. Day?
      b. Night?

12. When is the AAF Form #23 used?

13. What is the AAF Form #23A?

14. What is a local Flying Area?

15. How many such areas has Chanute Field?

16. What is the PIF?

17. What is the meaning of the following symbols on the Form 1A?

      a. Red dash?
      b. Red diagonal?
      c. Red Cross?

-1-

Flying regulation exam

Flying Regulations Examination Cont'd.

18. What must be done by the pilot prior to a flight when the plane is on a red dash or diagonal?

19. What is the pilots advisory service?

20. How are runways marked?

21. What is the basic index number of an airplane (B-17)?

22. What is the Form "F"?

23. What are the restricted areas within the local Flying Areas of Chanute Field?

24. How do aircraft enter the Chanute Field traffic pattern?

25. What is the meaning of the various light signals; in flight and on the ground?

26. What A.T.C. Center controls north bound flights out of Chanute? South bound?

27. What is the Chanute Radio Range Frequency?

28. What is the Chanute Tower Range Frequency?

29. What is the instrument approach procedure at Chanute Field? Give in detail.

30. What airports have been cleared for strange Field landings for airplanes from Chanute.

31. Chanute Field has an Auxillary Airport. Where is it?

References: AAF Forms 60-1, 60-5, 60-6, 60-9, 60-16, 60-20, 62-5, 62-16, PIF and Chanute Field Flying Regulations.

-2-

Flying regulation exam

HEADQUARTERS
ARMY AIR FORCES PILOT SCHOOL (SPECIALIZED FOUR-ENGINE)
OFFICE OF THE DIRECTOR OF TRAINING
CHANUTE FIELD, ILLINOIS

August 18, 1943

SUGGESTED METHODS OF ABANDONING AIRPLANE

B-17 E

A. GENERAL

1. Warning Signals.

There are three means enabling the pilot to communicate with the crew:

      a. The Alarm Bell
      b. The phone call light
      c. The interphone.

For emergency purposes the alarm bell should be used in a prescribed manner which is thoroughly understood by all crew.

The phone call light and the interphone may be used to supplement the bell signal when advisable, however, they should not be relied upon alone.

All signals are given by the pilot. If a commander is present, he will direct the pilot to give the desired signals.

2. Location of Signals.

There are three (3) alarm bells installed; one in the Bombardier's Compartment, one in the radio compartment, and one in the lower gun compartment.

There are four (4) phone call lights; three (3) adjacent to the alarm bells and one in the tail gunner's compartment.

Nine (9) interphone stations are located as follows:

        Bombardier
        Navigator
        Pilot
        Co-Pilot
        Upper gun turret
        Radio Operator
        Radio Crew
        Lower Gun compartment
        Tail gun compartment

The control toggle switches for the alarm bells and the phone call lights are on the pilot's switch panel.

-1-

Instructions for abandoning aircraft pg 1

B-17F QUESTIONNAIRE

NAME *GLENN H. ROJOHN*   DATE *January, 22, 1944*

1. (a) In what order should the engines be started, both electrically and manually? *#3, #4, #1, #2*

   (b) Why? *Start #3 first to keep from washing #3 engine cyl... walls down in event of primer leaking*

2. (a) Can wheels and/or tail wheel be retracted or extended independently of each other? *or how done manually*

   (b) Together? *Electrically*

3. Give various steps in feathering a propeller in *#4. ① Prop in low pitch*

   (a) Emergency. *① Cut generator of engine ② ...... ③ supercharger ...* *② Crack throttle ③ Hold feathering switch down until 800 Rpm as indicated*

   (b) Practice. *① Close throttle ② ......* *④ Mixture automatic rich ⑤ Cylinder head temp to 80°*

4. Give various steps in unfeathering propeller. *② Resume power setting desired*

5. Should engines be started with surface controls locked? *No*

6. What is total oil capacity? *148 gal.*

7. (a) What is normal fuel capacity? *1700 US gal.*

   (b) What is maximum fuel capacity? *3600 US gal.*

   (c) What is bomb-bay fuel capacity? *820 US gallons*

   (d) What is Tokyo Tanks' fuel capacity? *1080 U.S gal.*

   (e) How is fuel in bomb tanks used? *Transfer pump*

8. (a) What is maximum allowable air speed at which flaps may be lowered? *147 mph*

   (b) What is the maximum allowable diving speed? *305 mph.*

9. (a) How many exits are available for emergency use? *Five*

   (b) Give location of each. *① main door ④ Tail door ② ... ③ ...*

10. (a) What types of fire extinguishers are used in this airplane? *Carbon Tetrachloride and CO2*

    (b) Give location of extinguishers. *On bulkhead in nose comp, beneath copilot seat, forward power turret*

11. Give procedure in case of engine fire in flight. *① Feather prop ② Close oil flaps ③ Turn off booster pump*

12. (a) How many emergency bomb releases are installed? *Two*

    (b) Give location of each. *On floor at pilots left. Floor at fwd end of bomb bay.*

    (c) Explain procedure of operation. *First pull opens bombay doors. Second pull drops all bombs*

B-17 questionnaire (test with his written answers)

13. (a) On what engines are vacuum pumps installed?

#2 & #3

(b) How can pumps be checked individually?

Check vacuum with selector valve on left then right

14. How is hydraulic pressure maintained?

Pressure operated solenoid engage electric hydraulic pumps

15. What is the emergency braking procedure?

Handle in roof of cockpit.

16. How is the emergency accumulator serviced?

Open star valve between accumulators

17. What is the use of the hand hydraulic pump?

To build up pressure in event of electric pump failure

18. Why should power be reduced after take-off before lowering propeller RPM?

To prevent excessive manifold pressure

19. Why is carburetor icing seldom found in pressure type carburetor?

Gasoline is injected below venturi.

20. (a) Should more than one starter be energized simultaneously?

No.

(b) Why?

Load on batteries too great

21. Why should landing gear retracting switch be turned off even though the retraction or extension has been completed?

To prevent burning out motor in event limit switch fail

22. (a) Should landing gear be retracted during practice take-offs and landings?

No.

(b) Why?

To avoid undue wear on landing gear

23. (a) What provisions are made for elimination of propeller ice?

Distribution of an alcohol and glycerin mixture along the

(b) Where are controls? *all propeller blades*

at left of pilot on floor.

24. (a) Describe briefly the autosyn inverters

Two devices. Under pilots seat and under co pilots seat

(b) Explain their use.

One to operate autosyn instrument and one for flourescent light

25. Name all the autosyn instruments.

Manifold pressure gage, tachometer, oil pressure gage, fuel pressure, oil temp gage, cylinder head temp, carburetor air temp, free air temp, fuel gage

26. By what methods can bomb-bay tanks be released?

By bomb release mechanism of the bombrack or emergency bomb release

27. (a) Where are life rafts carried?

One on each side of the top bomb bay faring

(b) Where are controls located?

Incerling of radio compartment

(c) Explain in detail the use and operation of these controls.

Pull release handles.

28. (a) When landing gear is operated manually, should assistance be given electrically?

No.

(b) Why?

Crank may spin and injure personnel

- 2 -

B-17 Questionnaire p.2

29. (a) What supplies pressure for supercharger regulators?

Engine oil pumps

(b) Where are supercharger controls located?

On central control panel

(c) How can operation of regulator control be checked with engine idling on the ground?

By operating observed by someone on the ground

30. If intercooler becomes coated with ice, how is this eliminated?

By moving intercooler heat to on position

31. What is the purpose of the large coil spring on the elevator controls?

As an aid in controlling elevators to maintain flight position

32. (a) Where is air for the supercharger obtained with carburetor air filter open?

Inside the wing through the filters

(b) Where is air for the supercharger obtained with carburetor air filter closed?

Through the opening in the leading edge of wing

(c) Why must they be turned off above 8000'?

To prevent turbo overspeeding and detonation

33. How are fluorescent lights operated?

Hold switch in start position two seconds. Release and allow to swing back to On position.

34. What must be done before energizing an engine externally?

Turn switch on rear of starter motor to OFF position

35. What is the location of the auxiliary power unit and for what is it used?

On floor by main door. As a source of electric power on ground

36. What will happen if sudden application of brakes is made at altitude or in cold weather on the ground?

Expander tube rupture.

37. What is the danger in taxiing with low or dead batteries?

Electric hydraulic pump will not maintain pressure.

38. If pitot tube ices what instruments will again operate if the airspeed-static-pressure alternate source switch is moved?

Altimeter, rate of climb.

39. Will range be increased by using less than four engines?

No, it will be decreased

40. In case of failure of electric fuel transfer pump, how can fuel be transferred?

Hand transfer system

41. What is the purpose of individual energizing and meshing switches for each engine?

In order to continue to energize while meshing

42. What units depend on the hydraulic pressure system for their operation?

Brakes and cowl-flaps

43. Except in an emergency, how many propellers should be feathered at one time?

One - to prevent overload of battery

44. What auxiliary equipment is lost by the failure of -

(a) #1 engine?

Generator

(b) #2 engine?

Generator, Vacuum pump & glycol pump

(c) #3 engine?

Generator, Vacuum pump

(d) #4 engine?

Generator

- 3 -

B-17 Questionnaire p. 3

45. Explain fuel system as follows -

    (a) How is fuel transferred from tank to carburetor?
By engine driven fuel pump

    (b) Can all or two engines use fuel from one tank?
No, each engine has separate fuel tanks

    (c) Can fuel be transferred from one to tank to another? If so, explain.
yes, by means of fuel transfer pump

    (d) How can fuel be pumped from left bomb-bay to #1 engine tank?
First pumped to a right hand tanks, then back to #1 engine tank

    (e) Why are fuel gauges less accurate in this type system?
Tanks are not baffled

46. (a) What is the maximum permissible gross weight of the airplane overloaded?
65,000 lbs.

    (b) What caution should be exercised when operating the airplane overloaded?
Use of all of field and maximum power for take-off

47. Should landing gear be retracted as soon after take-off as possible?
Yes, except when practicing landings

48. (a) When and why do you turn on electric fuel booster pumps?
When starting engines for pressure at carburetor, high altitudes, take-off

    (b) What booster pump must be on in order to prime any engine?
 # 3

    (c) Why should primer (hand) be in off position when priming is completed?
To prevent overpriming

    (d) When are booster pumps turned off?
Between one and ten thousand ft.

49. Why is throttle pumping harmful in starting high pressure carburetor engine?
It causes back-fire hazards

50. (a) How should engines be started?
Regular starting procedure prescribed

    (b) How should engines be stopped.
Give stopping procedure

51. Why should engines be idled at 1200 RPM a short time before stopping?
To reduce cylinder head temp. and properly scavenge oil

52. What is engine RPM, manifold pressure, and carburetor mixture adjustment for the following:

    (a) Climb and high speed?
2300 rpm, 38 in. Aut rich

    (b) Cruising (desired)?
2000 rpm, 29 in. Aut lean

    (c) Cruising (maximum)?
2100 rpm 30 in Aut lean

    (d) Cruising (long range)?
at 5000 ft, 52,500 gross / 1630 rpm 28 in Aut lean.

53. What is cylinder head temperature for the following:

    (a) Maximum allowable for take-off and climb (5 min. max. time)?
260°C

    (b) Continuous operation (Rated power)?
218°C

    (c) Continuous operation (Cruising power)?
205°C

- 4 -

B-17 Questionnaire p. 4

    (a) Desired?

       75 lbs/sq. in

    (b) Maximum?

       80 lbs/sq. in

    (c) Minimum?

       70 lbs/sq. in

    (d) Minimum idling?

       15 lbs/sq. in

55. What is fuel pressure in lbs/sq. in. for the following:

    (a) Desired?

       12 to 16 lbs/sq. in

    (b) Maximum?

       16 lbs/sq. in

    (c) Minimum?

       12 lbs/sq. in

56. What is the oil inlet temperature for the following:

    (a) Desired?

       70° C

    (b) Maximum?

       88° C

57. What is the fuel consumption per engine per hour for the following:

    (a) Climb and high speed?

       110 gal

    (b) Cruising (desired)?

       49 gal

    (c) Cruising (maximum)?

       62½ gal

    (d) Cruising (long range)?

       38 gal.

58. Should engine controls be shot away, what predetermined position will your controls assume? *Throttles wide open, Supercharger 65% power, carb. temp cold. Engine Rpm 1850*

59. How is manifold pressure set for take-off when supercharging is desired? *Open throttle on one engine at a time to full open position, set supercharger regulator to desired manifold pressure.*

60. (a) When is oil dilution system used? *In cold weather when engine are stopped long*

    (b) Explain operation. *With engine running push dilution switched for a period not more than two minutes*

61. What is the first action in case of a runaway supercharger or propeller? *Throttle engine back*

62. What effect do the fumes from carbon tetrachloride fire extinguishers have on humans? *These fumes, known as Phosgene gas are poisonous*

63. How are ailerons locked? *By manual locking pin through the control column*

64. What are the various normal design bomb loads? *2064 lbs*

65. What is the maximum bomb load possible:

    8-1600 lbs. bombs inside

    2-4000 lbs. bombs outside

-5-

B-17 Questionnaire p. 5

66. Where is the main supply tank for the hydraulic system located?
On right rear bulkhead in pilots comp.

67. Name three ways pilot can attract attention of various crew members?
1. Interphone 2. Alarm bell (3) Phone call (a signal light)

68. Why can the radio compass be used satisfactorily during periods of intense static?
Loop antenna is shielded.

69. When using radio for beam flying, why should volume on the interphone control box be kept at a minimum?
If the volume is high it will act as an automatic volume control.

70. (a) Describe effectiveness of the various controls as the airplane approaches a stall.
Controls lose effectiveness in following order - ailerons, elevators, and rudder.

    (b) Why should one hand be kept on the throttles when taking off and landing?
To be able to apply power instantly.

71. What compartment is most desirable for storing weight with regard to the center of gravity?
Radio compartment, and compartment under pilots floor if not loaded.

72. Describe the procedure to be followed when a forced landing is to be made on water.
Use normal procedure prescribed in answer sheet.

73. (a) In case of radio failure and inverter stoppage after taxiing out, what is likely to be the trouble?
Low batteries.

    (b) What is the procedure in this case?
Notify tower and run up engines fast enough to cause ___

74. What is the number of available spaces for passengers and crew?
There are six assigned spaces for normal crew. There are ___ assigned spaces for normal crew plus ___

75. Pilots will be required to demonstrate (while in the airplane to the check pilot) that they have satisfactory knowledge as to the location of the following instruments:

    Life raft control

    Emergency bomb releases

    Hydraulic supply tank

    Fuel transfer valves and switch

    Propeller anti-icers, control and switch

    Wing de-icers, valve

    Aileron tabs, control

    Elevator tabs, control and lock

    Rudder tabs

    Cabin air control

    Vacuum pump selector valve

- 6 -

B-17 Questionnaire p. 6

WAR DEPARTMENT
AAF Form No. 83
(Approved 10-1-43)

4416

WAR DEPARTMENT
ARMY AIR FORCES

(To be filled in by check pilot)

QUALIFIED _____

UNQUALIFIED _____

PILOT INSTRUMENT CERTIFICATE APPLICATION AND FLIGHT CHECK FORM

Application

Application is hereby made for Instrument Pilot Certificate { AAF Form 8 (white) / ~~AAF Form 8A (green)~~ } (Strike out one.)

Name _Rojohn, Glenn H._   Rank _2nd Lt_   Organ. _232 CCTS_

Pilot rating _1-7-44_   Total Instrument Pilot time _50_

Instrument Pilot time last 5 years: Under hood _50_   Actual _____   Total _50_

The above is true to the best of my knowledge and belief.

Signed _Glenn H Rojohn_

Rank _2nd Lt A C_

Date _4-13-44_

Check Pilot Flight Test Report
(See reverse side for description of maneuvers)

Maneuvers	Satisfactory	Unsatisfactory
1. Instrument take-off	Cw	
2. Spiral climb	Cw	
3. Level flight	Cw	
4. 90° and 180° turns	Cw	
5. Steep banks	Cw	
6. Stalls	Cw	
7. Recovery from unusual maneuvers	Cw	
8. Glides	Cw	
9. Radio range orientation and low approach	Cw	
10. Position plotting by intersection	Cw	
11. Aural null orientation and homing	Cw	
12. Radio compass low approach	Cw	

NOTE.—To qualify for Instrument Pilot Certificate, AAF Form 8 (white), the applicant must satisfactorily complete maneuvers Nos. 2 to 9, inclusive, except that in the case of combat crew pilot in OTU and/or RTU organizations having radio compasses as standard equipment on their aircraft, maneuver No. 9 may be omitted. To qualify for Instrument Pilot Certificate, AAF Form 8A (green), applicant must satisfactorily complete all maneuvers.

This is to certify that I have personally flight-checked the above applicant on _B-17 F_ aircraft and find him qualified—~~unqualified~~.

Signed _O M Slaughter_
(Authorized check pilot)

Rank _Capt AC_

Date _April 11, 1944_

(Applicant must qualify "Satisfactory" on each separate maneuver)

16-27052-1

Pilot Instrument Certification

SEPARATION — ARMY QUALIFICATION — RECORD

LAST NAME - FIRST NAME - MIDDLE INITIAL	ARMY SERIAL NUMBER	GRADE	DATE OF ENTRY INTO ACTIVE SERVICE	SEX	DATE OF BIRTH
RO JOHN GLENN H	0819322	1st Lt	7 Jan 44	M	6 Apr 1922

PERMANENT ADDRESS FOR MAILING PURPOSES (Street and Number - City - County - State)
Box 145 Greenock Pa

CIVILIAN EDUCATION

HIGHEST GRADE COMPLETED	LAST YEAR OF CIVILIAN DANCE	HIGHEST DEGREE RECEIVED	MAJOR COURSE OF STUDY	NAME AND ADDRESS OF LAST SCHOOL ATTENDED
College 1½ yrs	1942	NG	Accounting	Robert Morris Sch of Acctg Pittsburgh Pa

OTHER TRAINING OR SCHOOLING

COLLEGE	NO. YRS	COURSE	COURSE	NO. MOS	COURSE	NO. MOS

SERVICE EDUCATION

SERVICE SCHOOL	COURSE	WKS ER KVS	RATING	ARMY SPECIALIZED TRAINING PROGRAM			
				INSTITUTION WHERE ENROLLED	CURRICULUM AND TERM (COURSE OF TRAINING PURSUED)	NO. OF WEEKS	GRADUATED YES NO
Maxwell Fld Ala	Pre-flt (P)	8		Dalhart Tex	Overseas Tng	4	
McBride Fld Chester Miss	Prim Pilot	8		Gulfport Miss	" "	8	
Malden Miss	Basic Pilot	8		Lanley Fld Va	Radar Nav Tng	6	
Stuttgart Ark	Adv TE Pilot	8					
Chanute Fld Ill	Trans B-17	8					

CIVILIAN OCCUPATIONS

MAIN OCCUPATION (TITLE)	SECONDARY OCCUPATION (TITLE)
Bank Teller	
JOB SUMMARY	JOB SUMMARY

NO. OF YEARS	LAST DATE OF EMPLOY-MENT	NAME AND ADDRESS OF EMPLOYER	NO. OF YEARS	LAST DATE OF EMPLOY-MENT	NAME AND ADDRESS OF EMPLOYER
1	1942	Union Natl Bk McKeesport Pa			

MILITARY SPECIALTIES

ASSIGNMENTS

YEARS	MONTHS	GRADE	PRINCIPAL DUTY	ARMY CODE NO	YEARS	MONTHS	GRADE	PRINCIPAL DUTY	ARMY CODE NO

SUMMARY OF MILITARY OCCUPATION AND CIVILIAN CONVERSIONS (shown by title)

Pilot: pilots aircraft and commands crew; inspects aircraft prior to flight; must have thorough knowledge of flight and navigation instruments, radio, meteorology, flying regulations and operation of engines.

Pilot: Commercial pilot

SUMMARY OF MILITARY OCCUPATION AND CIVILIAN CONVERSIONS (shown by title)

IF ORIGINAL IS LOST OR DESTROYED, NO REPRO-DUCTION IS POSSIBLE; NO COPY IS RETAINED BY THE WAR DEPARTMENT.

* THIS INFORMATION BASED ON SOLDIER'S STATEMENT. (Indicate by * any items not supported by military records)

DATE OF SEPARATION	SIGNATURE OF SOLDIER	SIGNATURE OF SEPARATION CLASSIFICATION OFFICER
27 Nov 45	Glenn H Ro john	O J SULIVAR 1st Lt A C

W.D., A.G.O. FORM NO. 100   15 July 1944

Separation papers

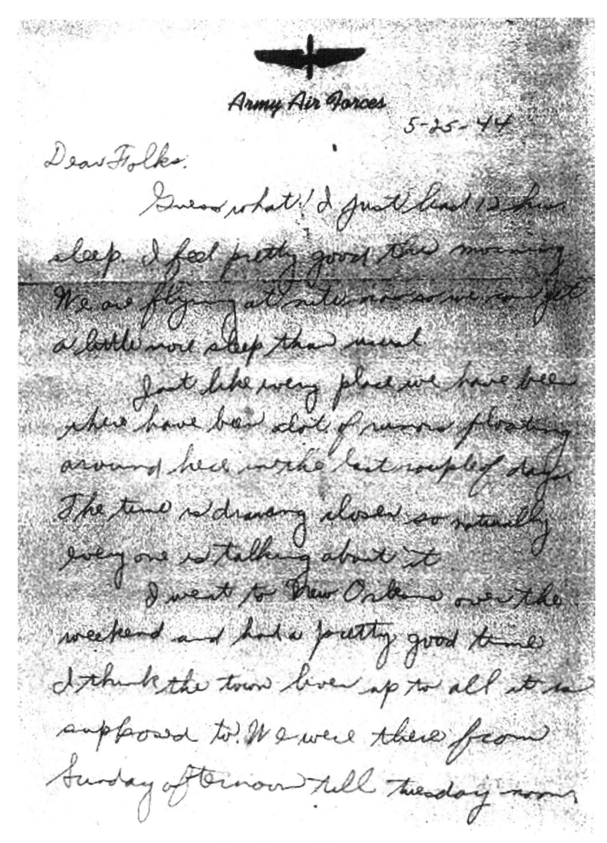

Army Air Forces

5-25-44

Dear Folks:

Guess what! I just had 13 hours sleep. I feel pretty good this morning. We are flying at nite now so we can get a little more sleep than usual.

Just like every place we have been there have been alot of rumors floating around here in the last couple of days. The time is drawing closer so naturally every one is talking about it.

I went to New Orleans over the weekend and had a pretty good time. I think the town lives up to all it is supposed to. W & were there from Sunday afternoon till tuesday noon.

The addresses of Glenn's Crew

things have been up around here except for being so darn hot. The weather as far as flying goes has been fine so we have flown every day. You ask for the addresses of my crew so I'll go and see if I can find them.

Hope everyone is fine at home. I haven't written any letter to anyone back there for awhile. Got a letter the other day from Bill Sandmeyer. He is only a couple hundred miles from here.

I'll bet the yard looks fine by this time. I sure would like to see it. Things looks much greener and more grass here than they were in Texas.

Well I wonder when this big invasion will come. I think things are getting pretty close to a head don't you. I guess we will find out soon enough.

Here are those names & addresses.

The addresses of Glenn's Crew

39

CHAPTER 4

GLENN H. ROJOHN'S JOURNEY AS A PILOT

Glenn's crew
Bottom row from left Neuhaus, unknown, Russo, Little
Top row Rojohn, Elkin, Horenkamp, Leek

Journey from the United States to England courtesy of Herman Horenkamp, tail gunner: See document at the end of the chapter.

July 2, 1944	Left Gulfport, Mississippi
July 4, 1944	Langley Field, Virginia
August 12, 1944	Grenier Field, New Hampshire
August 18, 1944	Meeks Field, Iceland
August 19, 1944	Valley, Wales

2nd Lt. Rojohn reported a concern that something didn't seem right on their trip from Iceland. It looked like they were going in the wrong direction. He asked his togglier, Elkin, to open his hatch to look at the stars. It was determined they indeed were off course. Rojohn and his crew made the necessary changes to be on track to England. Research reports that the Germans did tamper with the compass to throw off track as many planes as possible, so they would run out of fuel. Their goal was to minimize the American bomber fleet as much as possible.

August 20, 1944	Stone England

Enlisted men went to one location. Officers went to another location

September 6, 1944	95th Bomb Group
September 14, 1944	Assigned to 100th Bomb Group Thorpe Abbotts

The Piggyback Flight families are grateful for the detailed logs of mission #1 through #21 of Navigator Robert Washington and Tail Gunner Herman Horenkamp sent to Glenn H. Rojohn that were used as the basis for this chapter. We are also thankful for Waist Gunner Roy Little's logs provided by his cousin Rich Hehn. The logs of pilot Glenn H. Rojohn were also used. Logs are shown when they were available.

NOTE: Glenn's mother was not in good health primarily because of having both of her only children as bomber pilots fighting in the European Theatre. Because of that, he wrote her almost daily, so she would know he was alive and well. Many letters were brief. In letters he used phrases of being tired and busy as code for being on a mission. He also referenced his brother's missions so his family would have an idea how many each had flown. Several of Glenn's letters are included in this chapter.

Rojohn Mission Log & Roy Little Mission log

Mission #1   October 6, 1944   7 hrs 15 min

Target: Berlin, F. W. 190 Engine Plant
Bombs: 5 1,000# general purpose bombs
Ship: #944

Flak was moderate and very accurate. 11 or 12 holes in ship.

35 Aircraft lost—they hit the last group that was lagging behind.

Rojohn wrote on October 10 "One of my men received a purple heart." Referring to Roy Little's eye injury.

Picture of Ship damage due to flak Courtesy of Herman Horenkamp

Mission #2   October 7, 1944   8 hrs 30 min

Target: Bohlen Leipzig Oil refineries
Bombs: 10 500# demolition bombs
Ship: #297

Flak was moderate but not accurate. The 100th Bomb group led the division. Hit secondary target. Gill took Little's place. Rojohn wrote a letter October 7 "Won't write much for a while. I am so busy this week I don't know what day. Guess you know what I have been doing." He noted he listened to the World Series.

Mission #3   October 8, 1944   6 hrs

Target: Mainz, tank factory
Ship: #944

Some flak and rockets but not accurate. Milk run. Gill as waist gunner–Little still grounded.

Mission #4   October 12, 1944   7 hrs

Target: Bremen, F. W. 190 plant
Bombs: 10 500# incendiary bombs
Ship: #297

Some flak and rockets but not accurate. Milk run. Broncco as spare gunner—Little still grounded.

Letter written 10/13 refers to him going to see his brother. It was their first connection since beginning their missions.

Brothers chance meeting in London

Mission #5   October 17, 1944   6 hrs 45 min

Target: Cologne, Marshalling yards
Bombs: 34 100# general purpose bombs, two 500# incendiary bombs
Ship: #994
Flak and rockets heavy, but far away. Bush is spare gunner—Little still grounded.

Mission #6   October 18, 1944   9 hrs

Target: Kassel, F. W. 190 engine plant
Bombs: 5 500# demolition bombs, 5 500# incendiary bombs
Ship: #994
Flak moderate but not accurate. Bush as spare gunner—Little still grounded.
Jewelry mission. We earned our Air Medal

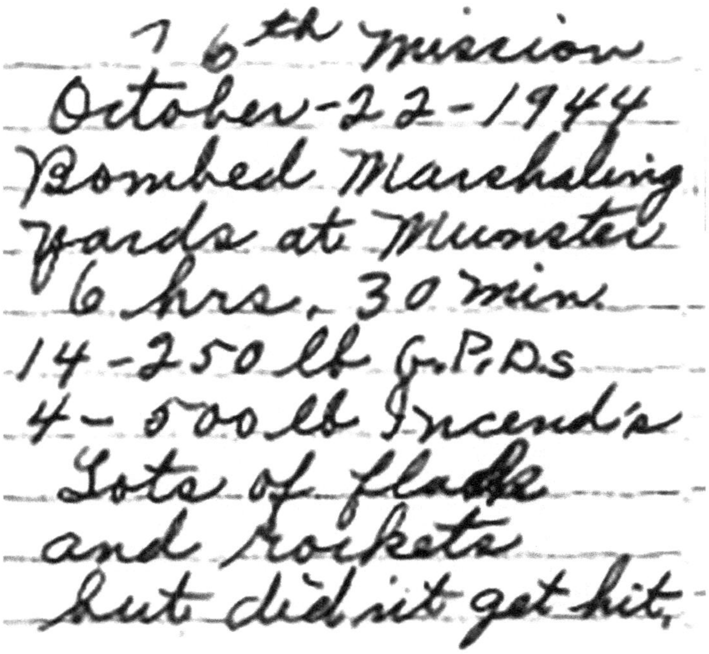

7 6th mission
October-22-1944
Bombed Marshaling
Yards at Munster
6 hrs. 30 min.
14 - 250 lb G.P.Ds
4 - 500 lb Incend's
Lots of flak
and rockets
but did not get hit.

Rojohn log

Mission #7   October 22, 1944   6 hrs 30 min

Target: Munster Marshalling Yards
Bombs: 14 250# general purpose bombs 4# incendiary bombs
Ship: #944
Flak light and below us. Little flying again.

Mission #8   October 30, 1944   4 hrs 30 min

Target: Merseburg synthetic oil refinery
Bombs: 250# general all-purpose bombs
Ship: #994
Recalled 1 hour 30 min before the target (Rojohn log says 70 min). No flak but saw a nice dog fight. No clipping from paper.

flack through my sleeve and Leek got hit under the seat,

9th mission November 4th – 44 Synthetic oil refinery at Meresburg. mission 7 hrs 45 min. 20 – 250 lb G.P.D.s We got it to day but good Bombing was visual and those ack ack boys shot hell out of us Picked up about eleven holes I got a piece of

Rojohn log he has misdated November 4

Mission #9   November 2, 1944   7 hr 45 min

Target: Merseburg Synthetic oil refinery
Bombs: 20 250# general purpose bombs
Ship: #994

Heavy flak. Damage accurate. Fighters hit a group behind us. Had to be 300-500 fighters. 11 holes in ship. Rojohn flak thru sleeve. Leek had flak hit under seat.

Promotion to 1st Lt.

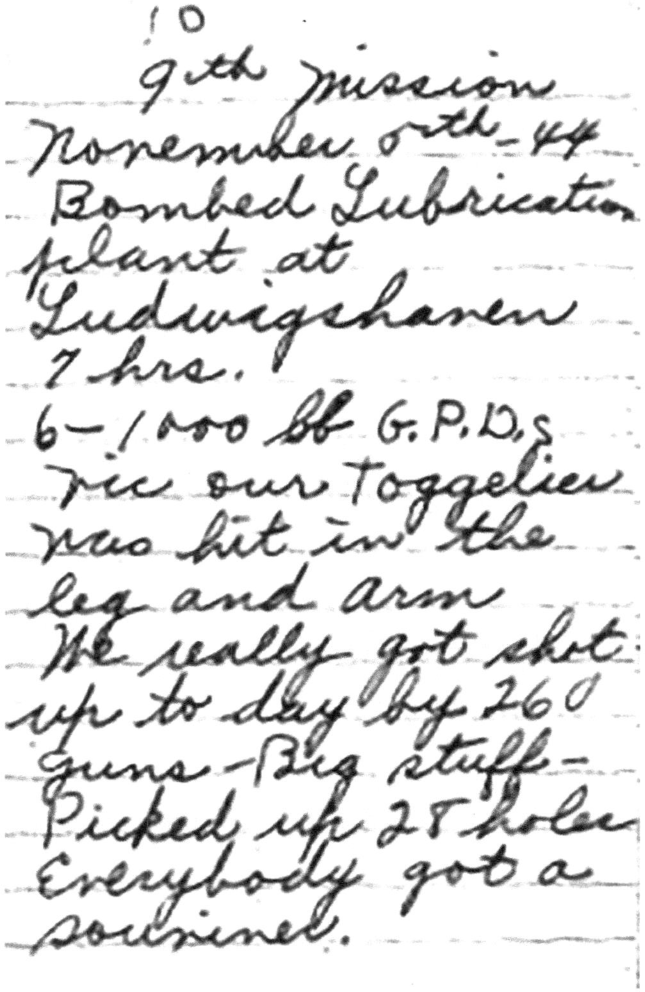

10
9th mission
November 5th – 44
Bombed Lubrication
plant at
Ludwigshaven
7 hrs.
6 – 1000 lb G.P.D,s
Vic our toggelier
was hit in the
leg and arm
We really got shot
up to day by 260
guns – Big stuff –
Picked up 28 holes
Everybody got a
souvinier.

Rojohn log

| Mission #10 | November 5, 1944 | 7 hrs |

Target: Ludgwishaven lubrication plant
Bombs: 6 1,000# demolition bombs
Ship: #994
Heavy flak and very damn accurate 28 holes in ship. Vic Vallerga togglier, wounded in arm & leg. 100th leading the division.

"Talking close to something big" November 5, 1944

10th mission
November 10–1944
Bombed airfield
at Wiesbaden
7 hrs.
38 – 100# lbs G.P.D.s
Bombs went
away when the
B.B. door came
open.
almost stalled out.

Mission # 11   November 10, 1944   7 hrs.

Target: Wiesbaden airfield
Bombs: 38 100# general purpose & demolition bombs
Ship: #994

No flak, a few rockets. Dropped bombs at I.P. When bomb doors opened a malfunction. We almost stalled. No holes in ship. More flak over England than Germany. Hans as togglier.

"Received Air Medal the other day. Wanted picture for the hometown paper"

Rojohn receiving Air Medal

Rojohn at Thorpe Abbotts

Rojohn and Leek at Thorpe Abbotts

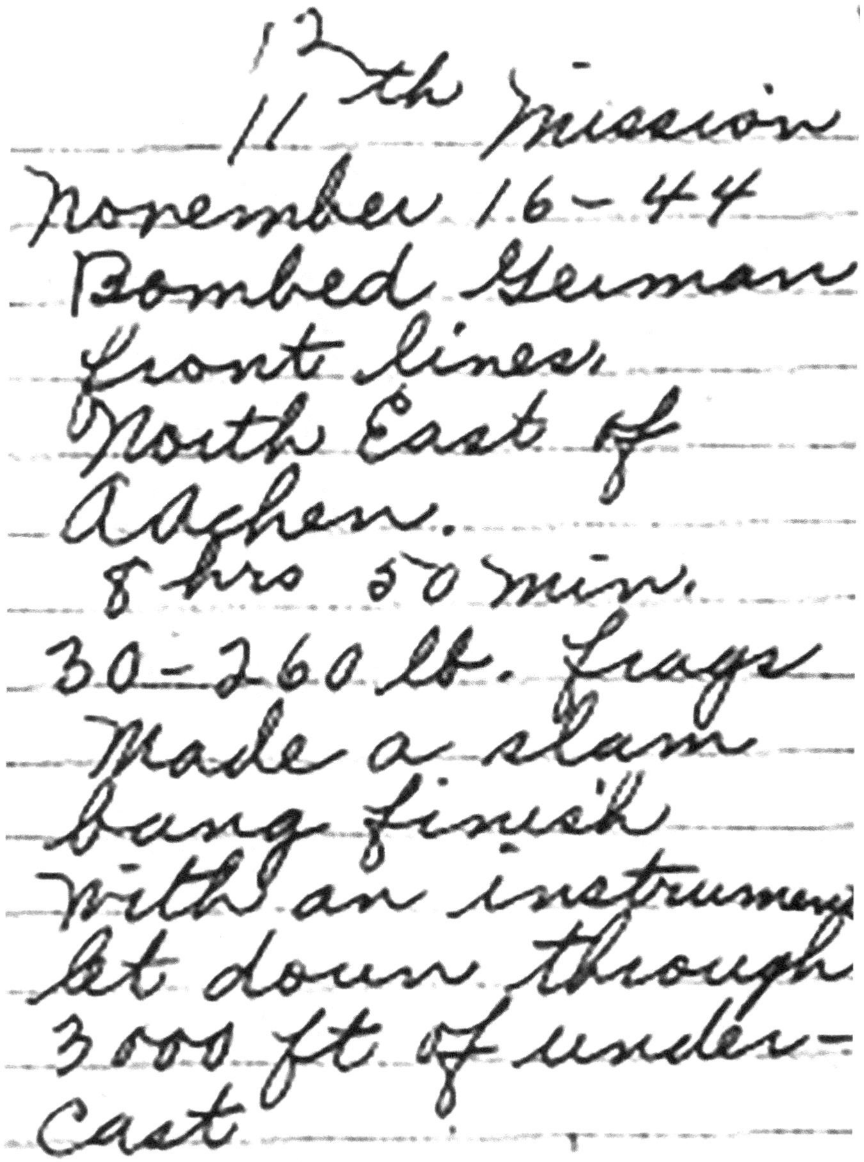

12
11 7th mission
november 16 - 44
Bombed German
front lines,
North East of
Aachen.
8 hrs 50 min.
30 - 260 lb. Frags.
made a slam
bang finish
with an instrument
let down through
3000 ft of under-
cast.

Rojohn log

| Mission #12 | November 16, 1944 | 8 hrs 50 min |

Target: German front lines between Eschweilera & Suren—Northeast of Aachen
Bombs: 30 260A fragmentation bombs.
Ship: #994
Very little flak & rockets.

Circled field for three hours, instrumental let down through 3,000' of undercoat 500' visibility. Little reported a slam, Bang finish.

13

13th Mission
November 21 — 44
Bombed marshaling
yard at Osnabruck
6 hrs. 45 min
12 — 500 lb — G.P.D.S

Weather kept us
off target.

Rojohn log

Mission #13   November 21, 1944   5 hrs 45 min

Target: Merseburg synthetic oil refinery. Clouds over target 28,00' so hit Osnaburch marshalling
            yards.
Bombs: Twelve 500# general purpose demolition bombs.
Ship: #944

Lots of flak & rockets, but only two bursts in formation. To meet 600-800 fighters but saw none. Brought bombs back. Malfunction in bomb bay.

Thanksgiving—"Sent air medal home"

14th Mission
November 27-44
Bombed marshalling
yard at Hamm.
6 chris.
6-1000 G.P.D.s.
mission to-day
took us to happy
valley.
Lots of rockets
some flak.

Rojohn log

Mission #14   November 26, 1944   5hrs 45 min

Target: Hamm marshalling yards
Bombs: six 1,000 general purpose demolition bombs
Ship: #944
Flak all over the place, but not much close to us. One hole in ship caused when flak fell, still sticking in wing.

"Guess reading about what is going on. I can't talk about it."

"Leonard 2/3 of missions." "I am more further behind" "Another crew got a purple Heart" (Vic Vallerga)

15th Mission
Dec 2 - 44
Mission was to
be rail yard at
Koblentz.
6 hrs.
12 - 500 lb. G.P.D's
mission was
scrubbed 2 minutes
from the I.P.

Rojohn log

Mission #15   December 2, 1944   6 hrs

Target: Koblenz Marshalling yards
Bombs: Twelve 500# general purpose demolition bombs
Ship: #944
Recalled 3 minutes before I.P. & 13 minutes before target. Milk run. 100th leading the division.

16th mission
Dec 4th – 44
Bombed Marshalling
Yard at Friedburg
8 hrs.
12-500 lb G.P.D.S
Flew 300 (ground space
target was to be
Giessen.
P.F.F. messed up
and we hit
Friedburg
All kinds of flak
and lots of rockets.

Rojohn log

Mission #16   December 4, 1944   8 hrs

Target: Friedburg Marshalling Yards
Bombs: Twelve 500# general purpose demolition bombs
Ship: #500 #944 grounded early, #3 engine wouldn't mesh

Flak all over the place but not much in our formation. PFF messed up. Giessen Marshalling Yards were the primary target.

crash landing
were also reported
missing
The Boys had our
clothes already.

17th mission
Bombed tank and
ordinance plant
at Berlin.
Dec 5 - 44.
8. hrs. 45 min.
20 - 250 lb G.P.D.S
They hit behind
us but too close
for comfort.
Spent 6 hrs on
oxygen
Temperture 45 below
at 28000 ft.
Hydraulic system
was shot out
Sweated out a

Rojohn log

12TH
DECEMBER 5. 1944
BOMBED TANK AND ORDINANCE
PLANT AT. BERLIN
MISSION 8 HRS 45MIN.
20. 250 LB. G.P.Os.
MISSION WAS TO BE POLITE BUT
TARGETS WERE CHANGED AT
BRIEFING. WE WORE BRIEFED FOR
1400 E.A. _ LUCK WAS WITH US
AGAIN AND THEY HIT BEHIND US
BUT TO DAM CLOSE FIR COMMORT.
SPENT 6HRS ON OXYGEN.
TEMPRATURE WAS 45 BELOW AT
28.000 FT. HYDRAULIC SYSTEM
WAS SHOT OUT_ WE SWEATED
OUT A CRASH LANDING_
WERE ALSO REPORTED AS
MISSING. THE BOYS HAD OUR
CLOTHES ALREADY.

Little log

Mission #17   December 5, 1944   8hrs 45min

Target: Berlin ordinance plant
Bombs: Two 500# incendiary bombs, Twenty 250# general purpose demolition bombs
Ship: #944
Briefed for 1400 fighters but none hit our group-saw a nice dog fight

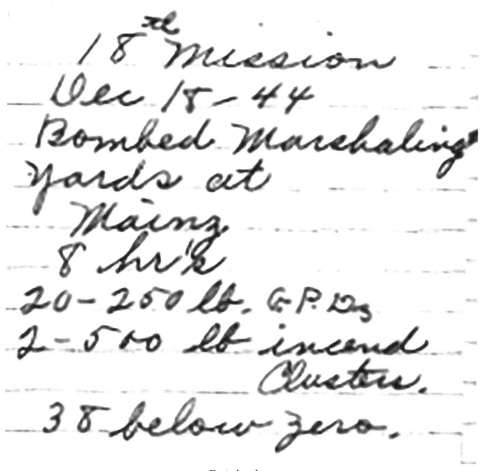

Rojohn log

Mission #18   December 18, 1944   7hrs 30min

Target: Mainz Marshalling Yards
Bombs: Two 500# incendiary bombs. Twenty 250# general purpose demolition bombs
Ship: #408 #944 went down in Brussels when we were on a pass. Started in high squadron &
ended in lead squadron—all messed up.
Saw no flak or fighters. Lead group failed to drop bombs. -38*

Christmas eve "On a pass Went to see Leonard then to London
Listened to Roosevelt Fireside chat Miss home."

19th mission
Dec 27 – 44
Bombed Marshaling
yard at
Fulda.
8 hrs
12 – 500 lb G.P.D's
Really plastered
the place
40 below zero.
Got my first
good look at
the front lines
Saw 3 little towns
blown right off
the map.

Rojohn log

Mission #19   December 27, 1944   8hrs

Target: Fulda marshalling Yards
Bombs: Twelve 500# general purpose demolition bombs
Ship: #408
No flak over target No fighters but briefed for 500. Flak & fire all over Germany. Flak over Belgium. Got good look at front lines. Saw 3 towns blown off map.

20th Mission
Dec 29 - 44.
Bombed Marshalling
yard at
Frankfurt.
7 hrs 45 minutes
Plenty of flak
but we led the
division and
they didn't get
our range until
we broke out
40 below zero.

Rojohn log

15th
December 29 - 1944
BOMBED MARSHALLING YARD AT
FRANKFURT
MISSION 7 HRS. 45 MIN. LONG
16 - 300 LB. G.P. Ds.
PLENTY OF FLAK BUT
WE LED THE DIVISION AND
THEY DIDNT HAVE OUR
RANGE UNTIL WE BROKE
OUT. PICKED UP A FEW
HOLES. ONE SHIP FROM
THE OUTFIT GOT AN ENGINE
SHOT OFF THE WING - THE
BOMBARDIER AND C.P. BAILED
OUT REST OF THE CREW
CAME BACK. LOTS OF
ROCKETS ASWE CROSSED
THE LINES. SAW ONE IT
BLOW UP, 40 BELOW ZERO

Little log

Mission #20   December 29, 1944   7hrs 45min

Target: Frankfurt Marshalling Yards
Bombs: Sixteen 300# general purpose demolition bombs
Ship: #408

Flak heavy over target. Pulled a surprise on them. No fighters but briefed for 300. Led division so out of range. Plane in formation had engine shot out. 4 holes in ship. -40*

12/29-- "Wonder what 1945 will bring. Hope the end of the war. Might not get a chance to write for a while."

Rojohn log

Mission #21   December 30, 1944   8 hrs.

Target: Kassel Marshalling Yards
Bombs: Twelve 500# general purpose demolition bombs
Ship: #408

Flak awfully heavy for 80 guns, flak all over the place but none in our formation. No fighters but briefed for 300-500 fighters.

There is an entry for the 22nd mission December 31, 1944 No notation when that entry was written or who wrote it.

Documents in Chapter 4

1. Original Horencamp Itinerary to Europe Assignment
2. Air Medal Documentation
3. Letter 10/10/44 pages 1-3
4. Letter 10/13/44 pages 1 & 2
5. Letter 11/3/44 pages 1 & 2
6. Letter 11/5/44
7. Letter 11/11/44 received Air Medal
8. Letter Thanksgiving pages 1& 2
9. Letter 12/1 pages 1 & 2 Vic Vallerga purple heart
10. Letter Christmas Eve pages 1- 3
11. Letter 12/29/1944

7-9-2000

DEAR GLENN,

I LOOKED TWICE THRU ALL MY ARMY STUFF AND CANNOT COME UP WITH THE NAVIGATORS NAME, I HAVE A PICTURE OF THE CREW THAT WENT OVERSEAS BUT NO NAMES. I THINK I GAVE YOU HIS LAST NAME ONE TIME BUT DID NOT HAVE HIS FIRST NAME,

LISTED BELOW IS ALL THE DIFFERENT PLACES WE WERE AT

4/5/44 TO 5-2-44   DALHART TEXAS
5-4-44 TO 7-2-44   GULFPORT MISS,
7-4-44 TO 8-12-44   LANGLEY FIELD VA.
8-12-44 TO 8-16-44   GRENIER FIELD N.H.
8-16-44 TO 8-17-44   GOOSE BAY LABRADOR
8-18-44 TO 8-19-44   MEEKS FIELD ICELAND
8-19-44 TO 8-20-44   VALLEY WHALES
8-20-44 TO 8-23-44   STONE ENGLAND
8-23-44 ENLISTED MEN WENT ONE PLACE AND OFFICERS WENT ANOTHER
9-6-44 TO 9-14-44   95TH BOMB GROUP
9-14-44 TO 12-31-44   100TH BOMB GROUP
I LEFT 100TH BOMB GROUP 1-17-45 FOR THE STATES

(OVER)

Horenkamp's Itinerary after left Langley page 1

62

THOUGHT YOU MAY WANT THIS INFORMATION.

PAULINE IS WRITING A NOTE TO JANE, I GUESS YOU COULD READ IT IF SHE LETS YOU.

Herman

Horencamp's Itinerary after left Langley page 2

OIC to the Air Medal
GENERAL ORDERS)   R E S T R I C T E D   Hq 3d Bombardment Division
                           ;   APO 559
NO.   1109   )   E X T R A C T   22 December 1944

    Under the provisions of Army Regulation 600-45, 22 September 194 , and pursuant to authority contained in letter 200.6, Headquarters Eighth Air Force, 23 September 1944, Subject: "Awards and Decorations," an OAK LEAF C___ is awarded, for wear with the Air Medal previously awarded to the follo__ named Officer, organization as indicated, Army Air Forces, United States Ar .

    Citation: For meritorious achievement while participating in he__y bombardment missions in the air offensive against the enemy over Continental __rope. The courage, coolness, and skill displayed by this Officer upon these __clons reflect great credit upon himself and the Armed Forces of the United States.

    GLENN H. ROJOHN   O-819322   1st Lt
    350th Bombardment Squadron, 100th Bombardment Group (H)

    By command of Major General PARTRIDGE:

OFFICIAL: N. B. H___LD,
                                                             Brigadier Gene___, U.S.A.
F. R. FITZPATRICK,   Chief of S___.
Captain, Air Corps,
Acting Asst. Adjutant General. R E S T R I C T E D

Air Medal Documentation

10/10/44

Dear Folks:

Didn't write last nite because I was pretty tired so I hit the old sack early.

Received the announcement today of Bessie' baby boy. Hope everything is fine. That is another new cousin. Will be anxious to see the little fellow. I bet Art is a proud papa. Had a letter from Rachel & Billy yesterday. Tell her thanks and I'll answer as soon as possible.

Say how did the horse show turn out. I bet it was

Letter 10/10 page 1

2

a nice affair. Am going to own a horse when we get back home. Remember how many years we almost bought one.

Now was glad to hear that you wrote to Mrs. Dees. She is a grand person. Hope sometime when we take a trip that you can meet her.

One of my men received the Purple Heart. Can't give you the details but everything is alright. Also all the gunners have received promotions so they are pretty happy now. You sent the list the other day

Letter 10/10 page 2

<u>3.</u>

of my new members. There are a few that are wrong. Richardson, Wogue & Jurst are no longer members. Will give you the other names in some other letter. Its time to close now. We are having ham for supper so I'm going now to eat. So long for now

Love,
Glenn

Letter 10/10 page 3

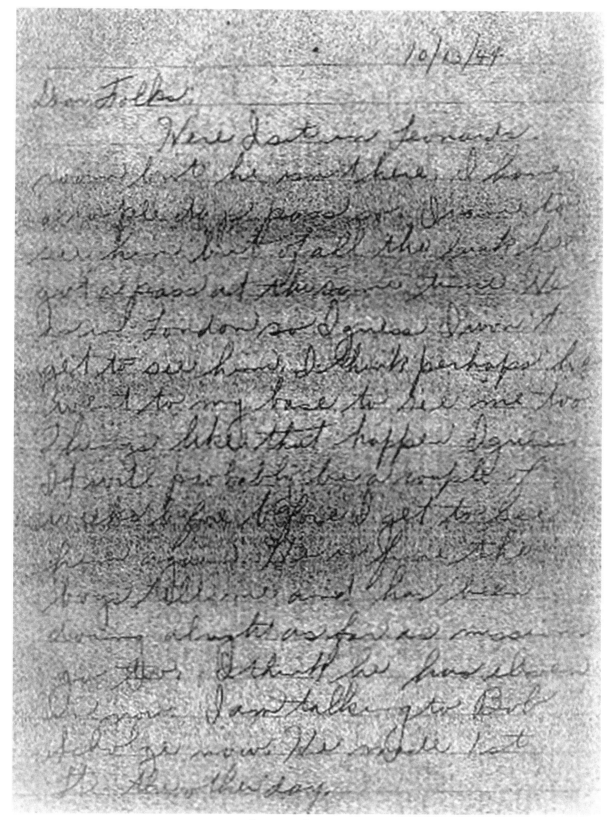

Letter 10/13 page 1

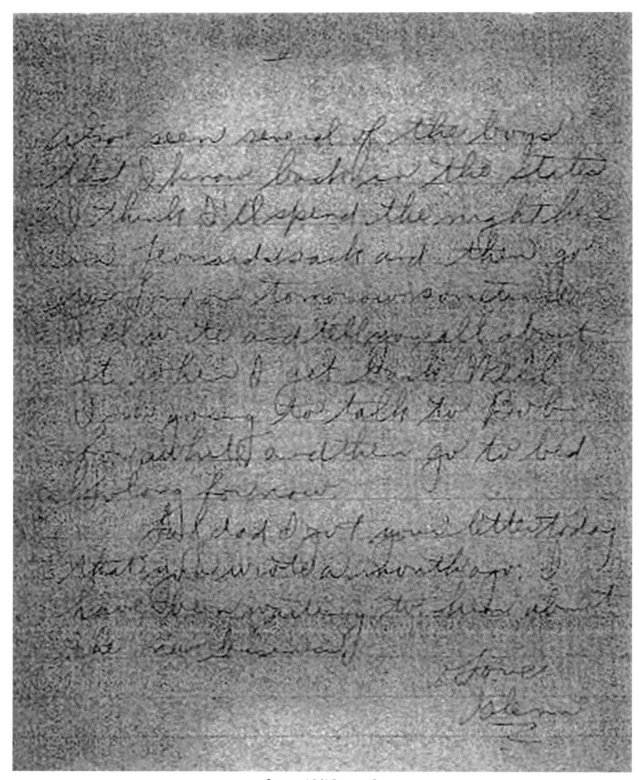

Letter 10/13 page 2

11/3/44

Dear Folks,

This is my first letter in a couple of days but I was a little too tired to write much. I sure hope you have received mail lately, I know what it is like to wait for mail. I had a letter from you all yesterday. Was sure glad to hear that you decided to continue with those treatments.

I want you to feel free to use that account of mine if you need it for those treatments. I want to see you fixed up. Really hope they help which I'm sure they will. Your nerves are the next important thing.

Letter 11/3 page 1

2.

I received a promotation the other day. I am now a 1st Lt. I haven't heard from Leonard for a few days but I suppose he is a 1st Lt. by now too.

Things have been O.K. Time is really flying isn't it? It will be Thanksgiving shortly now. Hope dad is enjoying his hunting. I suppose he and Clarence are still going to town with the furnace selling. Give everyone my regards. Say what do you think I should give the baby? Would you make out a check for her bank account? Whatever you think. I'll close for now. Will write again tomorrow.

Love.
Glenn

Letter 11/3 page 2

11/5/44

Dear Folks;

Just a short note tonight before I crawl in the sack. I am really tired tonight. Went to church this evening and had communion. That is the first for a good while.

I sure hope you all have gotten some mail by now. Its a shame that it is held up like that. Ours is about the same. I guess we will just have to be patient about it.

Well in a couple of days it will be election. I wonder who the victor will be. Some think it will be a pretty close race.

I am hoping to get down to see Leonard again tomorrow. Haven't heard from him for awhile. I guess he has been busy too. Enough for this note. Will write tomorrow.

Love.
Glen

Letter 11/5

11/11/44

Dear Folks:

Well here it is Armistice Day. I bet you were hunting today Pop Hope you had some luck. How are the dogs holding out. I shot a little skeet today. I like to do that. We can shoot anytime we aren't busy. No mail today again. It must be held up again somewhere. I took some pictures of the gang etc today. Will send them when I get them printed. Also had my picture taken. I received the Air Medal the other day so they wanted a picture for the Hometown paper. Everything is still OK. Will close for tonight. Will write again tomorrow.

Love
Glenn

Letter 11/11 received Air Medal

11/23/44
Thanksgiving

Dear Folks:

Another Thanksgiving day almost over. I attended church this morning and it was a very nice service! We have a lot to be thankful today I guess even though conditions are as they are. Leonard and I are safe and in good health plus everything else. Hope everyone is fine back home. I guess they had a nice church service at home this morning.

I hope the old man had a nice day of hunting today. Next year dad I hope to be right along with you and Clarence. All those eats that mother puts in that lunch basket sure sounds good.

Letter Thanksgiving page 1

73

2

I had your letter that you wrote on Armistice Day yesterday. That was pretty good time.

After church this morning I ate a wonderful dinner. Turkey and all the trimmings. It sure was good. Its amazing that they could put out such a dinner over here. I loafed around all afternoon. Played some cards etc. Had another package today. This time from my friend in Malden, Mo. By the way don't send that stationery I ask for just yet. Have gotten quite a bit of it lately. Well folks going to write a couple more letters so I'll close for now. Goodnite.

Love.
Glenn

P.S. I sent a box today with my air medal in it look for it

Letter Thanksgiving page 2

12/1/44

Dear Dad:

Just a note to you now. I just wrote mother a fairly long letter. Received a couple of letters from you in the last say week. Was very glad to hear about the hunting trips. Sure hope it won't be long till I'm there with you to help miss them. So you used my Winchester. I always told you that was a good gun.

Also glad to hear about the business. Hope you continue to give me all the news about that.

I went to see Leonard the other day. He is fine and I think he is a rest home now. He has almost ⅔ of his missions in. I'm some behind him but will catch up soon. It will be some

Letter 12/1 Vic Vallerga purple heart page 1

time yet before they are finished
I guess.

I am enclosing your Xmas
gift from us. I couldn't find anything
over here so I want you to get whatever
you need. We shall have a big Xmas
the first year we are home and really
have a party. So long for now dad
and keep up the good work.

I had another boy get the Purple
Heart but all is well. Don't worry
about us. I know it is natural but
I hope mom isn't worrying too much
Son
Glenn

I received my first full months pay Today
as a 1st Lt. and it was a good bit bigger.
I hope my allotments are coming through
OK. So to keep a check on it will you
GWR

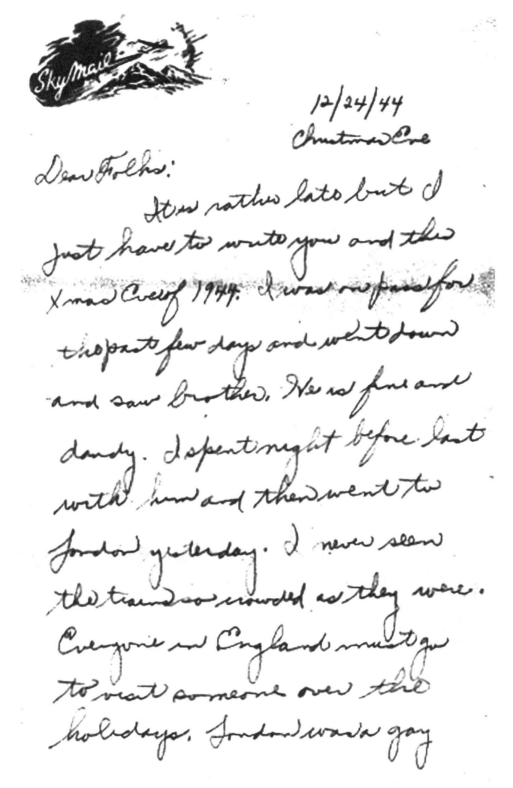

12/24/44
Christmas Eve

Dear Folks:

It's rather late but I just have to write you and the Xmas Eve of 1944. I was on pass for the past few days and went down and saw brother. He is fine and dandy. I spent night before last with him and then went to London yesterday. I never seen the trains so crowded as they were. Everyone in England must go to visit someone over the holidays. London was a gay

Letter Christmas eve page 1

2

place without everyone as happy as possible under the circumstances. Saw another stage play. It was very funny.

I got back in camp in time today to go to a Candle light service this evening held in the base Chapel. It was one of the most impressive services that I ever attended. We sang Christmas Carols and a choir made up of some of the men at the field sang. It was beautiful. The Chaplin had a very nice talk.

Letter Christmas Eve page 2

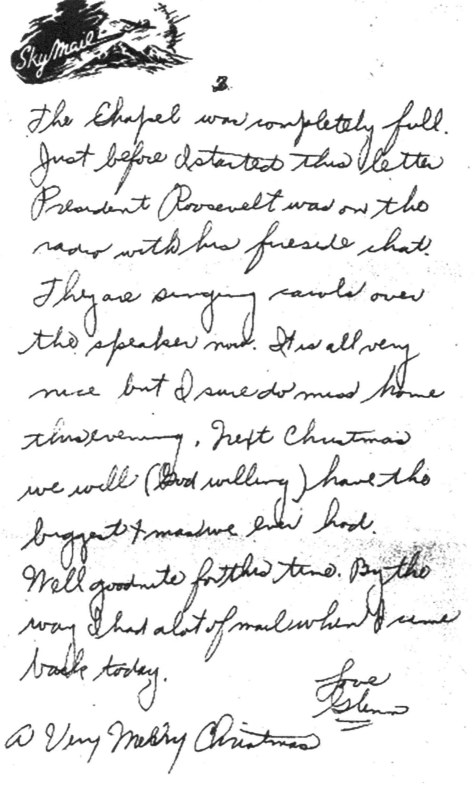

The Chapel was completely full. Just before I started this letter President Roosevelt was on the radio with his fireside chat. They are singing carols over the speaker now. It is all very nice but I sure do miss home this evening. Next Christmas we will (God willing) have the biggest & maddest we ever had. Well goodnite for this time. By the way I had a lot of mail when I came back today.

A Very Merry Christmas

Love
Glenn

Letter Christmas Eve page 3

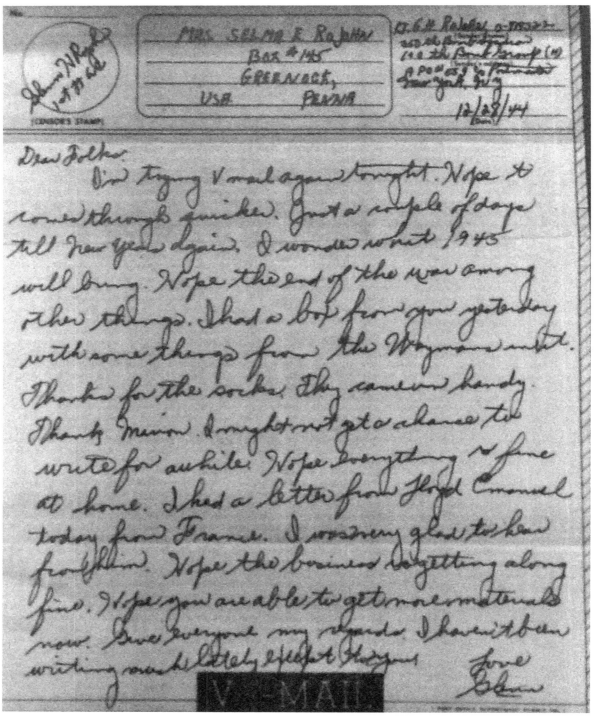

Letter 12/29

CHAPTER 5

MISSION 22 DECEMBER 31, 1944

December 31, 1944 was to be a day off for the Lt. Glenn H. Rojohn crew. Soon a much-needed trip to the "Flak House", a hotel like residence for rest and relaxation. Dreams of rest faded at 2 am. The Lt. was wakened. "My day off." He mumbled. "Maximum effort." was the response.

Everyone attended the briefing to learn the destination of the day. Then the crew gathered for their 22nd mission. They had a different ship to fly that day. #408 had not been repaired since the crew wasn't scheduled to fly that morning. The Little Skipper #42 31987 was their plane for the day. As they started to board, Lt. Rojohn noticed his tail gunner, his friend Herman Horencamp wasn't with the rest of his crew. He was told that he was in sick bay with frostbite. His replacement was Sgt. Francis Chase. They shook hands and boarded for the flight just like any other day.

According to The Army Air Forces in World War II: Combat Chronology, 1941-1945 Carter/Mueller, the Office of Air Force History and The Mighty Eighth War Diary by Roger A. Freeman the mission that day was oil industry targets at Hamburg; Wilhelmsburg refinery at Hamburg,; Grassbruk refinery at Hamburg; Mesenburg refinery; industrial area at Wenzendorf; and Hamburg. Targets of Opportunity were Stade and Nordholz Airfields and Heligoland Island. 1327 bombers and 785 fighters flew that day facing 150 Luftwaffe fighters.

Major C A Martin led the mission that day.

Leading the High Group C was Major Harry Cruver flying with Charles "Hong Kong" Wilson. Cruver's squadron memo for that day was sent to Rojohn after the war. In that memo he reported:

"Most of my Twenty-three missions were flown in bad weather, where we were either in the "soup" or in dense contrail accumulations, with highly restricted visibility. Hamburg was different—it was clear as a bell."

"The target planners at the Eight Air Force always arranged to have the attacking planes from the initial point to the target, fly on a course down-wind, or with a clear tail wind. On this occasion. We had a high velocity tail wind, over 300 miles per hour. So, we were able to move relatively rapidly on the bomb run. But no fighters were observed at the I. P., so I instructed the formation to bomb by individual squadron rather than by group salvo." "This was a mistake, because shortly after the I.P. swarms of FW190's and ME 109's concentrated their attacks directly on the dispersed formation during the bomb run. In addition to the vicious fighter attacks, the anti-aircraft fire was extremely accurate in the clear sky conditions during the bomb run. Many B-17s lost their power in one or more engines and became additional targets and easy prey for the fighters."

"At bombs away, the planes remaining descended 1,000, but then a strong velocity wind slowed all the 100th's planes to a ground speed of less than 100 miles per hour. (I believe the post mission critique recorded the ground speed at around 90 miles per hour) thus we were exposed a much longer time to the result of flak damage and in turn to fighter attacks as we proceeded at a snail's pace North to the coast in the Bremershaven area."

"Shortly after the target, I learned that all ammunition had been expended so the returning planes were really "sitting ducks" for the Luftwaffe. The formation of the remaining Square D planes became noticeably tighter to constitute a smaller target for the continuing fighter activity."

Lt. Glenn H. Rojohn flying, in C Squadron reported about that day:

"We turned South to Hamburg. We were flying at about 26,000 feet and going to the target having a 80 mile an hour tail wind, which got us there in a hurry. Over the target the flak was very heavy. We dropped bombs on target and then for some reason turned 180 degrees and started toward the North Sea. The tail wind we had going in was now a head wind at 80 miles an hour. Our ground speed at that point wasn't much over 70 or 80 miles an hour – giving the flak gunners and a little later the fighters a real field day."

Lt. William Leek, Rojohn's co-pilot reported:

"We turned south off the North Sea and headed for Hamburg. The target and the sky over it were black from miles away. The flak was brutal. We flew through flak clouds and aircraft parts for what seemed like an hour. When we passed the flak, we turned west. One of the crew said he was glad to see our fighter escort at last. Above us was a cluster of circling contrails. I remembered that our "little friends" flew parallel to us about 1000 feet higher. We turned North. Over the intercom I heard a yell that these B_____s were shooting at us. He was right."

The Operation Narrative for 31 December 44 sent to Rojohn after the war documented:

100th Bomb Group was the 7th in the Third Division column. Bombers were on a mag heading of from 320* to 325* when the enemy aircraft made their attacks from 5 to 7 o'clock high. The formation was good and tightened up when the bandits were reported. However, there were stragglers due to flak over the target. The enemy aircraft near the R.P., as the group was forming and made from 1156 hours to 1210 hours and from 5320N-0930E to 5330N-0910E. Formation was at approximately 25,000 feet altitude. Crews believed their escort was engaged in dog fights several miles distant while the enemy fire pressed their attacks. There were mainly FW 190's with very few ME 109's and two jet propelled ME 262's with a total of 50 enemy aircraft in various attacks which were made by single enemy aircraft or in pairs. Most of the enemy aircraft pilots seemed to be very skilled.

Rojohn commented later in speeches that "the fighters were so close he could see their faces." Years later in a conversation with a German friend, he told him The Little Skipper (not sure if meant formation) was attacked by two ME 262 jet fighters.

His co-pilot William Leek reported: "I had been at the controls during the bomb run. Glenn and I alternated the controls each half hour so that the man resting could enjoy the view. On this mission the lead plane was off Glenn's wing, so he flew the bomb run. I should have kept the controls for at least a half an hour, but once the attack began, our formation tightened up and we started bouncing up and down. Our lead plane kept going out of sight for me. I may have been over-correcting, but the planes all seemed to bounce at different times. I asked Glenn to take it and he did. In the cockpit we could hear our fifties firing and I think Russo yelled that he had a sure hit. I'd forgotten that our guns could be "felt" as well as heard. They felt good. A FW190 went by close to my wing and I remember thinking it could use a paint job. Two others joined it and they peeled off to the right for another pass. This was a long trip. When we finally reached the North Sea, we turned back to England. I am sure that we were still under attack. We always called for a condition check to each position when we got into the clear. We did not call that day."

The Operation Narrative reported the fighter escorts made rendezvous but were out of sight from shortly thereafter the enemy aircraft attacks. Then four P-51's and four P-47's were seen.

The 100th A group flying lead lost 3 aircraft – Williams, Henderson, Wilson. The 100th B Group Flying High lost 4 aircraft – Mayo, Carroll, Morin, Blackman.

The Planning for Mission 31 December 1944 of Headquarters Eight Air Force AAF Station 101 APO 634 documented the accounts from C Squadron. A/C # 43-38408 was first observed at 14,000 feet. Later it was seen to go into a tight spin at about 5,000 feet.

One or two chutes were seen. A/C #43-38436 (Webster) was shot up by enemy aircraft. A/C peeled out of formation to the right, went down in flames and exploded on the ground.

Based on all reports the Rojohn family have read, plus an interview with Ralph Christensen Co-Pilot of Mikesh's crew that is documented (document 20), and letter from George Rubin [document 19], due to the number of downed planes those still in the air were tightening up the formations as best as they could. Meaning the initial formation [Document 18] was altered as they were moving to tighten up.

Two additional planes went down that day. #42 31987 and #43 38547 were involved in an incident that would defy all odds. An anomaly of aviation occurred in the sky over the North Sea. Many variations of the story have been reported and several accusations have been made. Based on evidence and eye witness statements, the Rojohn family feels the true story of The Little Skipper and Nine Lives can be told.

A/C # 43-38436 piloted by Webster was spiraling to the right in flames leaving a hole in Squadron C formation. Rojohn attempted to radio about position. No answer. Later reports tell that probably the radio waves were jammed due to the amount of activity at that time. Not making any connection, he continued to fly to fill the position voided by Webster's downed plane. On a report of December 31, 1944 about Lt. Glenn Rojohn, it was documented that Pilot Ethan Porter immediately shouted a warning via radio. Grant Fuller was in the tail of Jones plane, #220P. "I wanted to yell at them to look out." Grant did not have access to a radio at his position. Paul Zak reported Rojohn was left and behind. Macnab was flying alone. According to Headquarters Eighth Air Force AAF Station 101 APO 634, at 1250 hours at 19,000 feet #457 and #987 pancaked together. Paul Zak reported (document 14) "Rojohn right engine began smoking with the two planes still together they begin a large circle to the left." Daniel Shaffer, substitute navigator on the Thomas Hughes plane, noted in his log for this mission – "Two 17s hooked together, 43-31987 piloted by Glenn Rojohn, having closed up into the space left by the loss of Lt. Webster. Unfortunately, B-17 piloted by William MacNab had risen slowly from below to fill the same position."

Jack Berkowitz, navigator on Nine Lives piloted by William Macnab, recollections of that day [Document 15]: "The first half of the mission was uneventful and normal. Our problems started when we turned North at the initial point and started back from the target. The wind was very strong and slowed the planes down to almost a walk. It was a clear day and the 88's coming from the ground were giving us trouble. At that time, we were attacked by ME 109's and FW109's and a few jet fighters. We tried to get over the North Sea because the enemy fighters would not follow us as a rule because of the gas shortage. As we were flying over the coast our wing man was hit. The pilot and co-pilot were killed, and I was hit in the leg." (document 9)

Later, reports came in after the mission and after the war ended that revealed the frenzy happening in the air. Planes were going down. Planes were being fired upon. Some planes were attempting to avoid enemy fire power, and some were jockeying to tighten a formation. [documents 15, 19, 20 from witnesses] In a phone interview Ralph Christensen, Co-Pilot of Lucky Lassie describes "We were Alternate Group Leader. We didn't move out of position. I watched as the planes jostled to tighten the formation around us." Documents report Rojohn piloting The Little Skipper and Macnab attempted to fill the empty slot created by either downed Henderson's or Webster's plane. According to Ralph Christensen, "Mik was flying so I had a full view of Rojohn crew forming on our right wing when I saw Macnab's plane pull up under Rojohn's plane." In a phone interview he described it as "Rojohn was in position to go home. Unfortunately, that didn't happen." From his vantage point 100' yards away, Grant Fuller described the planes as "not a crash but melding of two planes." That correlates with what Jack Berkowitz, Navigator of Macnab's crew, reported— Macnab and Vaughn had been hit or suffered damage by enemy fire. They were slumped in their seats, no longer flying the plane.

The crews of both planes didn't know what happened. They just heard a thud, a lot of noise and a lot of confusion.

Lt. Glenn H. Rojohn's, Pilot of The Little Skipper, recollection of what happened: "We had moved in to fill a position of a downed B-17 when all of a sudden it happened. A crash-a lot of noise and confusion. We then realized we had collided with another plane. Our ship immediately began to fall out of control. Not knowing at the time that the other B-17 was still attached to us, Bill and I with a lot of brute strength managed to level the plane enough to permit the crew to bail out. One of my engines was on fire, so my co-pilot and I shut down the engines of my plane to save from their being more fire. This happened out over the North Sea about 25-40 miles.

Lt. William Leek, Co-Pilot of the Little Skipper, recollection of what happened: We had not been on a westerly course very long when our lives were abruptly changed. I think the other B-17 came up underneath us because we lunged upward. The two planes ground together like "breeding Dragonflies". Glenn's outboard prop bent into the nacel of the lower plane's engine. Glenn gunned our engines two or three times to try to fly us off. It didn't work, but it was a good try. The outboard left engine was burning on the plane below. We feathered our propellers and rang the bail out bell. The two planes would drop into a dive unless we pulled back all the time. Glenn pointed left and we turned the mess toward land."

I remember our father saying "I didn't want to go into the water. I knew we wouldn't survive. I wanted to make it to land."

Ed Woodall, ball gunner on #43-38457 Nine Lives, recollection of that day [Document 16]: "We were lead for the high flight of the low C Squadron. Our wing men were #43-38408 piloted by Leo Ross and #43-3846 piloted by Charles Webster. Following the bomb drop, we were attacked by fighters near the R. P. and lost Webster followed by Ross. As a result, we were flying alone. At the time of impact, we lost all power, and intercom on our aircraft, I knew we were in trouble from the violent shaking of the aircraft, no power to operate the turret, loss of intercom, and seeing falling pieces of metal. My turret was stalled with the guns up at about 9 o'clock. This is where countless time drills covering emergency procedures from the turret paid off. I automatically reached for the hand crank, disengaged the clutch and proceeded to crank the turret and guns to the down position so I could open the door and climb into the waist of the plane."

Robert Washington, Navigator of The Little Skipper, recollection of what happened: "After we crossed over a little town of Aurich and across the coastline near Norden, we started our let-down and I gave a sigh of relief, thinking about making such good ground speed as we turned Southwest. When we hit the other plane below us, the bombardier (James Shirley) and I just looked at each other and did nothing for what seemed like a long time. I opened the escape hatch and saw a B-17 hanging there with three engines churning and one feathered. I believe Rojohn and Leek banked to the left and headed back East toward land. The bombardier and I crawled up into the pilot's compartment and saw the two of them holding the wheels against their stomachs and their feet propped against the instrument panel. They feathered our engines to avoid fire, I think."

Orville Elkin top turret gunner's recollection of that day: "A wave of Glenn's hand meant bail out. I went to the waist of the plane and secured a chute from our spare bag of gear. S/Sgt. Joseph Russo was trapped in the ball turret. S/Sgt Roy Little, Neuhaus and myself took the hand crank for the ball turret and tried to crank it up. It wouldn't move. His machine guns were jammed between the ribs of the plane below us. There was no means of escape. Little, Neuhaus and I made our way to the side door escape hatch."

Leek report about the bail out: "We got over land and Shirley came up from below. Bob Washington came up and was just hanging between our seats. Glenn waved them back with the others. We were dropping fast." I could hear Russo saying his Hail Mary's over the intercom. I couldn't help him. I pulled off my helmet and noticed that we were at 15,000 feet. Glenn told me to follow Bob but I refused. I was sure that a man who was 24 years old was not strong enough to hold the planes level while I went through the bomb bay to the escape hatch. If the planes went into a spin, escape would not be possible. I stayed along for the ride."

Bob Washington recollection about the bail out: The bombardier and I went thru the bomb bay and out the waist door, careful to drop straight down in order to miss the tail section of the other plane which was a little to the right of our tail. We were well over land at this time. The bombardier was coming down behind me."

Lt. Glenn H. Rojohn recollection of that time: "If I were to let go of the controls, the plane would start to spin and no one could get out. Elkin and the boys in the back bailed out over the water. Washington and Shirley were standing behind Bill and me and waited a few minutes to go after we crossed land. At this point all the exits were blocked. The door at the rear waist was clear. I knew Bill and I had to go all the way back there to get out and by that time the plane would be in a tight spin and spin us in the plane. I ordered Bill to go. I would try to hold the two planes level while he bailed. He refused. He told me "We are riding this out together" "He saved my life."

There were numerous reports from witnesses seeing chutes floating in the air. Most saying they saw 6.

Ed Woodall, ball turett gunner of Nine Lives remembers his experience: "I made a very poor landing on the beach and was dragged inland by a very strong gale-like wind. As a result of my 'crash landing' I suffered broken bones in my right foot and a fracture of my right hip and pelvic bone which made it impossible for me to collapse my chute. I was finally stopped when it became tangled in a fence. I was immediately picked up by a home guard and taken to a small village."

Jack Berkowitz, navigator of Nine Lives, remembered: "We were over the North Sea. I left from the escape hatch in the nose of the plane. We jumped and free fell to get below the fighting. Luckily the wind was in our favor and it took us onto the beach."

Bob Washington remembers bailing out: "Descending in my parachute, I turned to watch the two planes locked together by the top turret guns of one and the ball turret of the other. My bombardier was coming down behind me. There was a stiff wind blowing. My chute caught on a utility pole. [Document 3] When I got out of my harness soldiers were running across a field. I made no effort to escape." German eye-witness Schmidt from Hohenkirchen was ice skating on a pond. His recollection was "The soldier (Shirley) landed on the frozen pond where I was skating only moments before. He was wounded in the shoulder. The second enemy was hanging on a lamp pole. (Washington)"

Reports state Elkin, Neuhaus, Chadwick and Comer landed in the North Sea close to shore, then captured. Neuhaus landed close to the Island of Wangerooge. Seyfried, Little, Chase, Ethridge and Rench landed in the North Sea, but were not recovered. German reports state one of those men's body was recovered. It is not known which one for sure, but a picture and conversation presumes it to be Rench.

The Pilot, Co-Pilot, and ball turret gunner were the only ones remaining in The Little Skipper.

Rojohn remembers: "The bottom plane was on fire. It was hot enough that the 50 caliber bullets were exploding around us. Three of the bottom plane's engines were still running. We feathered our engines to reduce the explosion factor. With three engines out of eight running, we were falling like a rock but holding level. It seemed like an eternity. We went into circles. I prayed. We didn't have a choice of a landing spot."

Co-Pilot Leek recalls of the final minutes: "We were shot at by guns that made a round of white puff like big dandelion seeds ready to be blown away. The fire was pouring over our left wing. I wondered what the German gunners thought we were up to and where we were going. Fifty caliber shells began to blow at random in the plane below. I don't know if it was the last flak had started more or if the fire had spread but it was hot down there. At one point I tried to beat my way out of the window with a veri-pistol. I still don't know why—just panic. Praying was allowed. We had our feet on the instrument panel for more leverage. Glenn seemed frozen. In one position. I hit him on the shoulder and screamed "Pull". We gave it one last effort and hit the ground."

A friend of Hans Jurgen Juergens, a German witness, stated "The Commander of the flak battery gave the order 'Stop shooting at these two hooked-up-planes immediately they have enough problems right now... they are coming down any way in a short time, save ammunition for more dangerous planes.' Those orders were not liked because they would miss the bonus points and furlough time for shooting down two planes."

Bob Washington said of his view when coming down in the sky: "I saw no more chutes. When the planes hit the ground, I saw them burst into flames and the black smoke erupting. It was an emotional sight for me. I had no idea or hope that Glenn, Bill, and Russo could survive."

(Document 1) Washington flight path to landing and coordinates of the landing

Many German officials and citizens witnessed the collision in the air and the landing. Among them were Battery Chief Oberleutnant Broderbeck, Firing Leader Feldwebel Ahrends and Rudolf F Skarwan, operator of optical range finder gunner. Obergefreiter Muller with powerful glasses gave a play by play description to those in the flak house of the crazy Americans flying 8 motors. He stopped watching when he saw chutes and focused watching for more. In a letter written decades after the incident, Rudolf F Skarwan quoted the A Team television show "I love it when a plan comes together." Bruno Albers, Hans Jurgen Jurgens and Adolf Bruns were also documented as witnesses.

Lt Glenn H Rojohn has said often in his many post war speeches: "We hit the ground. As we did we slid off the bottom plane and kept on going. We knocked down an empty German WAC's home."

Drawing by Bruno Albers

THE PIGGYBACK FLIGHT PILOT'S JOURNEY

Nine Lives exploded when the two planes hit the ground. All that was left of The Little Skipper was the nose, the cockpit, and the seats they were sitting on. Unfortunately and unceremoniously, Joseph Russo was killed in the explosion at landing. To Bob Washington's horror, as he was floating in the sky he saw the flames and the black smoke fill the sky.

15-20 grueling minutes is the estimated time frame given by historians and pilots for the flight of two planes stuck together from collision to landing.

In Terry Flatley's short story Breeding Dragonflies over the North Sea she quotes Leek: "When my adrenalin began to lower, I looked around. Glenn was OK, and I was OK and a convenient hole was available for a fast exit. It was a break just behind the cockpit. I crawled out onto the left wing to wait for Glenn, pulled out a cigarette and was about to light up when a young German Soldier with a rifle came slowly up to the wing making me keep my hands up. He grabbed the cigarette out of my mouth and pointed down. The wing was covered with gasoline."

The legendary, historical mid-air collision of The Little Skipper and Nine Lives will be forever known as the Piggyback Flight. It was a miracle that anyone survived. Unbelievable to anyone who witnessed the event that the two pilots of The Little Skipper walked away from landing of the two B-17s stuck together with not more than a few scratches.

Joe Urice, 100th Bomb Group Veteran who was still alive at this writing, said of this day: "That 31 December 1944 day of a mission to Hamburg was a sad, unforgettable day for the 100th and all involved."

Herschel Whittington commented about the incident, "Many of the Hundredth's anguished fliers saw the two fortresses cling... riding pick-a-back... the two bombers squirmed, wheeled in the air, trying to break the death lock." 12 planes in the Bloody 100th were lost December 31, 1944 and 111 airmen KIA or MIA.

Contrails My War said it best "There have been amazing stunts pulled in the colorful and courageous history of man's will to fly, from days of Daedalus and DaVinci to the days of the brothers Wright and Billy Mitchell, but none more strangely heroic than the day Rojohn and Leek safely crash landed their two planes pick-a-back on a field in North Germany.

Crew Members and Witnesses

Lt. Glenn H Rojohn Crew

Lt. Glenn H. Rojohn--Pilot

Lt. William Leek--Co-Pilot

Roy Little--Waist Gunner

Joseph Russo--Ball Gunner

James Shirley--Bombadier

Orville Elkin--Togglier

Sgt. Francis Chase—Tail Gunner
Top Right on Wall of Margarten

Missing photos of Bob Washington—Navigator and Ed Neuhaus—Radio Operator

Herman Horenkamp—Tail Gunner 21 missions

Lt William Macnab Crew – Nine Lives

Lt William Macnab – Pilot

Ed Woodall – Ball Gunner

Jack Berkowitz – Navigator

Francis Seyfried – Tail Gunner

Missing Nelson Vaughn, Co-Pilot, Ray Comer Bombadier, Joseph Chadwick, Toggelier,
Henry Ethridge, Radio Operator, and Duane Rench – Waist Gunner.

Witnesses

Ralph Christensen and Ramon Conjeco

Grant Fuller

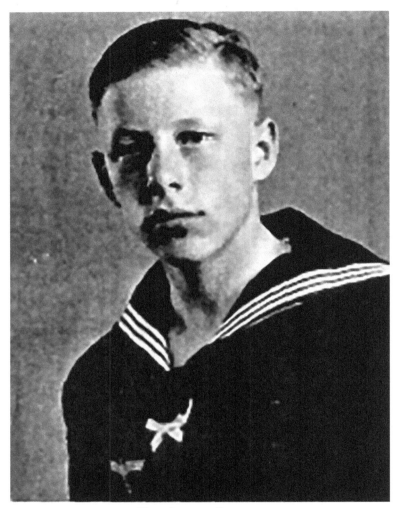

Hans Juergen Juergens
Navy AA Gunner (Eyewitness) 1943/44
Navy 1944/45

Bruno Albers
Navy AA Enemy flight control 1944   Luftwaffe 1945

Rudolph Skawran
Navy AA Gunner (Eyewitness) December 1944

Documents in Chapter 5

1. Flight Path as per Bob Washington
2. Volker Urbansky coordinate points
3. Note hanging on pole as per Bob Washington & Bob Washington Map
4. Rojohn Crew 12/31/44 documentation
5. Macnab Crew 12/31/44 documentation
6. Major Cruver Remarks
7. Glenn H Rojohn report for 12/31/44 pages 1 & 2
8. Operation Narrative pages 1- 4
9. Lt. Glenn Rojohn Report
10. German Witnesses Log
11. German Operation Center drawn by Bruno Albers
12. German Flak House drawn by Bruno Albers
13. German witness statement
14. Paul Zak letter pages 1& 2
15. Jack Berkowitz letter pages 1 & 2
16. Ed Woodall letter pages 1 - 3
17. Grant Fuller Letter
18. 12/31/44 formation drawn by Grant Fuller
19. Rubin Letter documenting collision
20. Ralph Christensen Letter documenting collision
21. Signed Bill Leek Letter documenting 12/31/44 pages 1 & 2
    Pictures of Crew Members and Witnesses

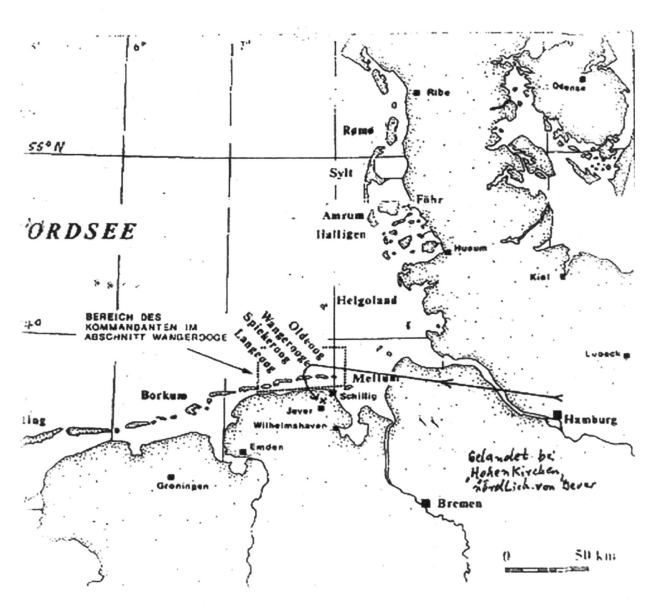

Path of return flight of The Little Skipper. Collision in the North Sea
off the shore of Wangerooge. Landing near Tetten Field

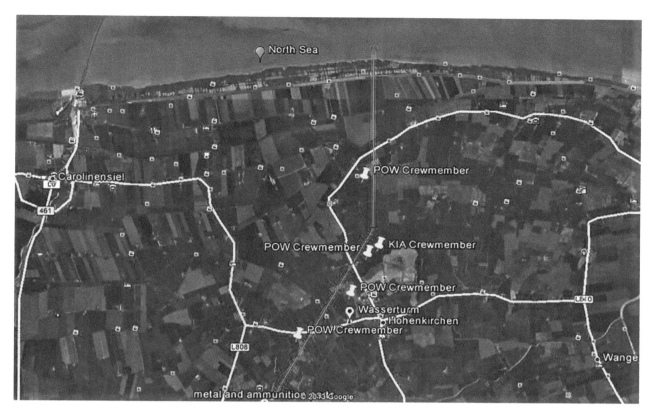

Volker Urbansky's points of discovery of the Piggyback Flight landing.

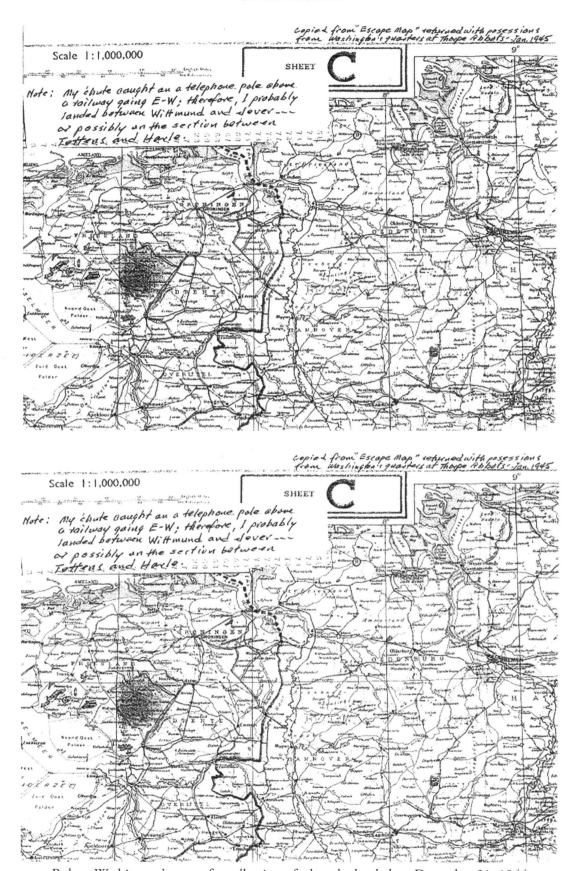

Robert Washington's map of recollection of where he landed on December 31, 1944

42.31987 LN-A "LITTLE SKIPPER" XR-A 172R GLENN ROJOHN
AIRCRAFT   LO-D ALT   WAS "SHILAYEEE" PRIOR TO 5TH JUNE 44   INIT NAME
CAC FLACK FIRE EXP (EOL)(CL) CTO MECH   11550 - 4246
                    9 MAR44 AOS   350/418 31 : DEC : 44   POW ST.
(MRR) SAL RZI INT ENEMY USE   SQD DAY MONTH YEAR

NOTES COLLIDED WITH 43-38457   241 HAMBURG
Both SHIPS TRYING TO FILL SAME   MISSION NR PLACE
Hole - And collided - Being called NOTES
Piggy Back And upset The GERMANS   SHIPS WERE AT 19000 FT
                                   Bombing Run AT 25000 FT.
                                   BURIAL OF KIA - AT WITTMUND-FR.
                                   27 MISSIONS

SC	CB	POS COMP	NAME	INT	RANK	STAT	REMARKS MID. RUSTRINGEN GER.
165	172R	P	ROJOHN	GH	LT	POW	
160	172R	CP	LEEK JR	WG	LT	POW	
169	173R	NAV	WASHINGTON	R	LT	POW	Replacement LNR on SHORE 27 MISSIONS SWA
155	172R	TTG	ELKIN	OE	T/S	POW	Landed 10 miles OFF SHORE
163	172R	ROG	NEUHAUS	EG	S/S	POW	Landed on island.
148	173R	BTG	RUSSO	JL	S	KIA	NOTHING FOUND OF BODY 22 MISSIONS
167	173R	BTG	SHIRLEY	JR	S	POW	Replacement- had on shore.
146	173R	LWG	LITTLE	RH	S	KIA	NOTHING FOUND OF BODY 17 MISSIONS
143	173R	TG	CHASE	FR	S/S	KIA	NOTHING FOUND OF BODY 1ST MISSION

AFTER LT WEBSTER went down. ROJOHN closed up in his space. - AT The SAME
Time WM MACNAB Rose slowly from below to fill the same hole. The ships collided
And Locked Together - with elevators and Ailerons still working - ROJOHN cut his
ENGINES and using 3 ENG of - MACNAB's 43-38457. They slowly Turned The A/C
Toward LAND ALL That could bailed out. ON Landing - ROJOHN's Ship slid off
OFF. while MACNAB's EXPLODED, 6 chutes were seen before Landing and most believed were
OVER-LAND.

- 31st DEC - 100TH SENT 3 GPS TO HAMBURG - 12 Planes Failed to Return - led by HARRY CRUVER
who Flew w/ HONG KONG WILSON. HAMBURG was clear. AS A BELL. MISSION FROM IP TO TARGET was
downwind 300 MPH GS. NO FIGHTERS in sight so GP was in Formed to bomb by SQDS - A mistake,
Shortly after bombs AWAY - SWARMS of FW190 AND ME109S hit the dispersed Formations. The
FLAK was EXTREMELY ACCURATE And many A/C were damaged And was attacked by E/C. AT
bombs. AWAY the GP descended 1000 FT And head winds slowed them down TO 90 MPH. AS
such the GP was Exposed to A much Longer FLAK barrage And E/C ATTACKS. AT A SNAIL
Pace to the COAST AT BREMERHAVEN. most ammunition have been Extended on the
RUN - So the A/C were sitting ducks for the LUFTWAFFE. AT THIS POINT All SQUARE D
PLANES Tightened Formations but too Late - 12 A/C were Lost - WILSON - ROSS -
MORIN - WILLIAMS - BLACKMAN - CARROLL - WHITCOMB - HENDERSON - MACNAB -
ROJOHN - WEBSTER. - 23 E/C destroyed - 8 damaged Probably destroyed. 11 damaged -
108 MEN Lost.

200

December 31, 1944 daily report of The Little Skipper/Glenn Rojohn crew

AIRCRAFT   ACC ART   2 SEP 44 AOS '''   PAGE   INIT NAME 11359 - 4180
EAC HACK FIRE (EXP)(CO)(EL) CTO MECH   350   31 DEC 4.4   KIA
                                              540   DAY MONTH YEAR ST.

(MIA) SAL RZI INT ENEMY USE   +   241   HAMBURG
                                   + +   MISSION NR   PLACE
NOTES COLLISION WITH 42-3198?   + +   NOTES
WAS TRYING TO FILL HOLE LEFT BY   1000 SQD   Bomb run at 25000 - ships
LT WEBSTER- CAME UP UNDER ROJOHN 13 BnGp   locked up at 19000~ Crossed
WHEN HAD SLID OVER TO FILL SAME SLOT. 3 DIV   coast at 10000 - CL
                                              COLLISION WAS OVER NORTH SEA NEAR
                                              FRISIAN ISLANDS. 25 TH MISSION

SC	CB	POS comP	NAME		INT	RANK	STAT	REMARKS
								CR- RUSTRINGEN GER
172	172M	P	MACNAB	.	WG	LT	KIA	wounded before collision
149	172M	CP	VAUGHN	.	NB	LT	KIA	wounded before collision
151	172M	NAV	BERKOWITZ	.	TACK	LT	POW	Replacement from charles wilson cr
153	172M	BCM	COMER	.	RE	LT	POW	Replacement from charles wilson cr
152	172MTTG	C.CHADWICK		.	JA	T/S	POW	
144	172M	ROG	ETHERIDGE	.	HS	T/S	KIA	drowned at sea
170	172MBTG	WOODALL	JR	EL	S/S	POW	TAPS - 5 FEB 94
148	172M	RWG	RENCH	.	DF	S/S	KIA	drowned at sea
		LWG						
148	172MTG	SEYFRIED	.	FJ	S/S	KIA	drowned at sea.

...as webster was shot down and left a slot in the formation. Rojohn slid over
And MacNab came up under him. Both were locked up. Rojohn cut engines and use.
MacNab's 3 ere maneuver both towards land. All bailed out that could. - 6 chutes
were seen. As the ships touched down - Rojohns slid off while MacNab's exploded.
Radio warnings were not heard in time to prevent collision.

31st Dec - 100TH sent 3 GAS to Hamburg - 12 Planes failed to return - led by Harry Cruver
who flew w/Hong Kong Wilson. Hamburg was clear as a bell. mission from IP to target was
downwind 300 MPH GS. No fighters in sight so GP was informed to bomb by Sqds- A mistake
shortly after bombs away.- swarms of FW190 and ME109S hit the dispersed formations. The
flak was extremely accurate and many P/C were damaged and was attacked by EAC. At
bombs away the GP descended 1000ft and head winds slowed them down to 90 MPH. As
such the GP was exposed to a much longer flak barrage and EAC attacks at a sn.
pace to the coast at Bremerhaven. Most ammunition have been expended on the
run- So the A/c were sitting ducks for the Luftwaffe, at this point all squared
planes tightened formations but too late - 12 A/c were lost. - Wilson - Ross -
yo - Morin - Williams - Blackman - Carroll - whitcomb - Henderson - MacNab -
Rojohn - webster. - 23 EAC destroyed - 8 damaged probably destroyed - 11 damaged -
108 men lost.

December 31, 1944 daily report of Nine Lives/Macnab crew

MAJ CRUVER. Remarks. 31 DEC 44. HAMBURG 31 DEC 44
Ro. JOHN - McNAB

Sqdrons->MEMOS   Page 1

MEMO

LED 100TH TO HAMBURG 31 DEC 44; WITH CHARLES (HONG KONG) WILSON CREW.
THE 100TH LOST TWELVE AIRCRAFT.

MAJOR CRUVER WRITES: "MY RECOLLECTION IS THAT THE PRIME TARGET WAS
NOT AN OIL REFINERY, BUT THE SUBMARINE PENS ON THE OUTSKIRTS OF THE
CITY.

I RECALL THAT MOST OF MY TWENTY-THREE MISSIONS WERE FLOWN IN
BAD WEATHER, WHERE WE WERE EITHER IN THE "SOUP" OR IN DENSE
CONTRAIL ACCUMULATIONS, WITH HIGHLY RESTRICTED VISIBILITY. HAMBURG
WAS DIFFERENT-- IT WAS CLEAR AS A BELL.

THE TARGET PLANNERS AT EIGHTH AIR FORCE ALWAYS ARRANGED TO
HAVE THE ATTACKING PLANES FROM THE INITIAL POINT TO THE TARGET, FLY
ON A COURSE DOWN-WIND, OR WITH A CLEAR TAIL WIND. ON THIS
OCCASION, WE HAD A HIGH VELOCITY TAIL WIND, OVER 300 MILES PER
HOUR, SO WE WERE ABLE TO MOVE RELATIVELY RAPIDLY ON THE BOMB RUN.
BUT NO FIGHTERS WERE OBSERVED AT THE I.P., SO I INSTRUCTED THE
FORMATION TO BOMB BY INDIVIDUAL SQUADRON RATHER THAN BY GROUP
SALVO.

THIS WAS A MISTAKE, BECAUSE SHORTLY AFTER THE I.P. SWARMS OF
FW 190'S AND ME 109'S CONCENTRATED THEIR ATTACKS DIRECTLY ON THE
DISPERSED FORMATION DURING THE BOMB RUN. IN ADDITION TO THE VICIOUS
FIGHTER ATTACKS, THE ANTI-AIRCRAFT FIRE WAS EXTREMELY ACCURATE IN
THE ABSOLUTE CLEAR SKY CONDITIONS DURING THE BOMB RUN. MANY B-17S
LOST POWER IN ONE OR MORE ENGINES AND BECAME ADDITIONAL TARGETS AND
EASY PREY FOR THE FIGHTERS.

AT BOMBS AWAY THE PLANES REMAINING DESCENDED 1,000 FEET, BUT
THEN A STRONG VELOCITY HEAD WIND SLOWED ALL THE 100TH'S PLANES TO
A GROUND SPEED OF LESS THAN 100 MILES PER HOUR. (I BELIEVE THE
POST-MISSION CRITIQUE RECORDED THE GROUND SPEED AT AROUND 90 MILES
PER HOUR) THUS WE WERE EXPOSED A MUCH LONGER TIME TO THE RESULT OF
FLAK DAMAGE AND IN TURN TO FIGHTER ATTACKS AS WE PROCEEDED AT A
SNAIL'S PACE NORTH TO THE COAST IN THE BREMERSHAVEN AREA.

SHORTLY AFTER THE TARGET, I LEARNED THAT ALL AMMUNITION HAD
BEEN EXPENDED SO THE RETURNING PLANES WERE REALLY 'SITTING DUCKS'
FOR THE LUFTWAFFE. THE FORMATION OF THE REMAINING SQUARE D PLANES
BECAME NOTICEABLE TIGHTER TO CONSTITUTE A SMALLER TARGET FOR THE
CONTINUING FIGHTER ACTIVITY. IT WAS A THIS POINT THAT THE
INCREDIBLE COLLISION OCCURRED BETWEEN MacNAB AND ROJOHN WHICH
CAUSED THEM TO CRASH LAND IN 'PIGGY-BACK' FASHION'
-30-

MAJ CRUVER - Remarks.   ROJOHN INCIDENT- 200-D

Squadron Memo December 31, 1944 Rojohn Incident, Major Cruver remarks

DECLASSIFIED
Authority: NND 735001
By: NARA NARA Date: 1973

AFPPA-13

CASUALTY QUESTIONNAIRE

550   40

1. Your name ROJOHN, GLENN. H   Rank 1st LT   Serial No. O-819342

2. Organization 100th Gp Commander JEFFRES Rank Col. Sqn CO LYSTER Rank Maj
(full name)   (full name)

3. What year 1944 month DECEMBER day 31 did you go down?

4. What was the mission, AIR ATTACK ,target HAMBURG ,target
time, 1030 ,altitude, 26000 route scheduled, THRU N. SEA
,route flown NORTH SEA THEN DUE SOUTH TO TARGET

5. Where were you when you left formation? BACK OVER NORTH SEA ON WAY BACK

6. Did you bail out? No

7. Did other members of crew bail out? YES, ALL BUT, PILOT, Co-PILOT
WAIST & BALL TURRET GUNNER

8. Tell all you know about when, where, how each person in your aircraft for whom no individual questionnaire is attached bailed out. A crew list is attached. Please give facts. If you don't know, say: "No Knowledge".
NO KNOWLEDGE OF EXACTLY WHERE ANY BAILED OUT. WE HAD
A MIDAIR COLLISION WITH ANOTHER SHIP OUT OVER THE NORT SEA
AS THEY STARTED TO BAIL OUT IMMEDIATELY SOME LANDED IN THE
WATER AND TWO WERE GLOWN TO LAND (SHIRLEY & WASHINGTON)

9. Where did your aircraft strike the ground? IN VICINITY FROM NORTH SEA TO
WILHELMSHAVEN

10. What members of your crew were in the aircraft when it struck the ground? (Should cross check with 8 above and individual questionnaires) PILOT & Co-PILOT
(NOT SURE IF BALL TURRET GUNNER WAS IN SHIP OR
NOT. I THINK HE WAS.

11. Where were they in aircraft? PILOT & Co-PILOT WERE IN PILOTS COMPARTMENT
FAIRLY SURE GUNNER WAS IN BALL TURRET

12. What was their condition? _____

13. When, where, and in what condition did you last see any members not already described above? IN Frankfort I saw all my crew members except
Reese, Gibb & Neel.

14. Please give any similar information of personnel of any other crew of which you have knowledge. Indicate source of information. None —

(Any additional information may be written on the back)

6-3642, AF

Lt. Glenn Rojohn Casualty Questionnaire as per his recollection and written by him

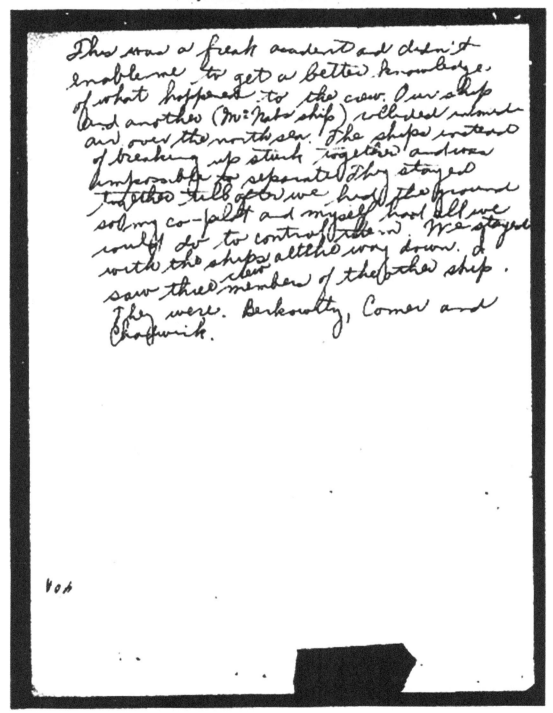

This was a freak accident and didn't enable me to get a better knowledge of what happened to the crew. Our ship and another (Mc Nab's ship) collided in mid air over the north sea. The ships instead of breaking up stuck together and was impossible to separate. They stayed together till we hit the ground so my co-pilot and myself had all we could do to control them. We stayed with the ships all the way down. I saw three crew members of the other ship. They were. Berkowitz, Comer and Chadwick.

Lt Glenn H Rojohn's Casualty Questionnaire p.2

OPERATIONAL NARRATIVE FOR 31 DEC 44 – HAMBURG :. 12 A/C LOST

S-2 Narrative

1-Photographs show visible bomb bursts from 100th "A" Squadron from 750 to 1500 yards NE of MPI. Poor bombing results.

Photographs show visible bursts from 3 A/C from 100 "B" Squadron to be 2000 yards SSW of MPI. Poor bombing results.

Photographs of 100th "C" Squadron show visible bomb bursts 500 yards NNW of MPI. Poor bombing results.

2-100th Bomb Group was the 7th in the Third Division column. Bombers were on a mag heading of from 320° to 325° when the E/A made their attacks from 5 to 7 o'clock high. The formation was good and tightened up when bandits were reported. However, there were stragglers due to flak over the target. The E/A attacked near the R.P., as the Group was forming and made attacks from 1155 hours to 1210 hours and from 5320N-0930E to 5330N-0910E. Formations were at approximately 25,000 feet altitude. Crews believed their escort was engaged in dog fights several miles distant while the E/A pressed their attacks. There were mainly FW 190's with a very few ME 109's and two jet propelled ME 262's with a total of 50 E/A in the various attacks which were made by single E/A or in pairs. Most of the E/A pilots seemed to be very skilled. A few seemed to be fairly green. There was nothing unusual about the enemy's armament or equipment. Most of their A/C were silver with red and black markings. A few had grey fuselages and yellow tails and a few were painted with a yellowish brown camouflage paint. All three squadrons plus the composite squadron were attacked. Nearly all passes came from high rear with the E/A passing through the bomber formation or breaking off short and diving below.Then they came in again, making pursuit curves and came in from high rear. Several B-17's were seen going down smoking and flaming.

3-Flak: Frisian Islands: Meager, distant.
Heligoland: Meager, distant.
Brunsbuttelkoog: Meager, pointed, inaccurate.
Hamburg: Intense-barrage and tracking. Usually large bursts and accurate.
Wessermunde: Moderate, tracking, accurate.
Nearly all flak damage came immediately after bombaway.
4-
Weather was 6 to 8/10 middle clouds on route in and back but CAVU over target.

5-All squadrons and three A/C of the composite squadron encountered E/A and the fighter escort was nil during the attacks. Fighter escorts made rendezvous but were out of sight from shortly thereafter till after the E/A attacks. Then four P-51's and four P-47's were seen.

100 "A" Squadron lost 3 A/C, one due to E/A and two due to a collision resulting from one A/C being hit by flak. WILLIAMS-HENDERSON-COL — WILSON-FLAK

100 "B" Squadron lost 4 A/C, three due to E/A and one due to a combination of E/A and flak. MAYO – CARROLL – MORIN – BLACKMAN

100th "C" Squadron lost four A/C, two to E/A and two as a result of a collision in which one rode the other pick-a-back to the ground. RO-JOHN –MAC-NAB
Composite lost one A/C to E/A. ROSS – WEBSTER
WHITCOMB

31 Dec. 1944

12 – CREWS – LOST
LT. W.G. MAC NAB – 168-B

Operation narrative for 31 Dec 44 – Hamburg

E. d. Woodall

Operational Narrative for 31 December 1944 Mission.

Target: Hamburg

1-General Narrative: Thirty-seven aircraft including three PFF
aircraft departed this base in formation at 0647-0737 hours. The
100th Bomb Group flew as the 13th "B" Group which was the eighth
group in the Division line. The 100th Bomb Group also furnished
three aircraft to fly as the high flight in the low squadron of
the 13th "A" Group.

2- Target: Primary target, Hamburg Oil Refineries were bombed
visually. Flak was extremely heavy over the target.

3-RP: As briefed. At this point enemy fighters attacked our formation. The formation was good and tightened up wh en bandits were
reported.

4-Aircraft not attacking:	"A" SQDN	"B" SQDN	"C" SQDN	COMP. ELE
A/C scheduled to take-off..	11 and 1	11 and 1	12 and 1	3
A/C dispatched.............	11 and 1	11 and 1	12 and 1	3
A/C attacking..............	10 and 1	11 and 1	11 and 1	3
A/C not attacking..........	1 spare	0	1 spare	0

100th "A" Squadron: A/C #42-31412 returned early with bombs. Spare.

100th "C" Squadron: A/C #44-8284 returned early. Crashlanded at Tib-
onham. Spare.

5-Losses: Twelve aircraft.
"A" Squadron: A/C #43-38124 was broken in two by collision with A/C
#066 which fell on it after A/C #066 was hit by flak. Both A/C went
down in flames. One chute was seen.
        A/C #42-31066 received a direct hit by flak just before
bombs away. Bombs were salvoed and the A/C fell off on right wing and
dropped on to A/C #124. Both went down flaming and one exploded.
        A/C #42-107233 was not seen and positively identified
after bombs away. However, an A/C believed to be #233 was seen trail-
ing after the E/A attack, losing altitude and smoking.
"B" Squadron: A/C #43-38381. The pilot of A/C #381 was heard on VHF
saying he had lost 2 engines and might lose a third. Expected to ditch
if he lost another engine. A/C was subjected to intense flak over
  rmershaven and was last seen over Speikeroog Is.
        A/C #42-31895 was seen to dive straight down at 1225
hours. The pilot recovered at 13,000 feet and when last seen was heading
in a westerly direction with all engines going.
        A/C #43-38459 dropped back and lost altitude after first
fighter attack.Pilot was heard on VHF at 1250 hours saying he had two
wounded aboard but might be forced to ditch. Said he would try to reach
Holland and that he had gasoline for one hour flying.
        A/C #43-38215 sustained a direct flak hit on #2 engine
which began to smoke and finally stopped. E/A attacked as it lagged.
One engine burst into flames and a moment later the A/C exploded.
One chute was seen.

"C" Squadron: A/C #43-38457. At 1250 hours and 19,000 feet, two (2)
B-17's believed to be #457 and #987 pancaked together, circled and
crashed, still attached to each other. Six chutes were seen before
the A/C landed and most of them are believed to have fallen on land.
there was no fire from the A/C in the air or on the ground, although
there was some smoke.
        A/C #43-38408. An A/C believed to have been #408 was
observed first at 14,000 feet. Later it was seen to go into a tight
spin at about 5,000 feet. One or two chutes were seen.
        A/C #43-38436 was shot up by E/A. A/C peeled out of
formation to the right, went down in flames and exploded on the ground.
        A/C #42-31987. At 1250 hours, at 19,000 feet, two (2)
B-17's believed to be #457 and #987 pancaked together, circled and
crashed, still attached to each other.

Composite Element: A/C #43-38535 was attacked by E/A, at 1200 hours.
The entire right wing began to burn and the A/C circled for two minutes under control before spinning down enveloped in flames. No chutes
were seen.

-Lead Bombardier, "A": The bombing run was visual. We picked up the
target area shortly after turning on the IP. The smoke screen proved
very effective at first but as we progressed along the bombing run
we were able to pick out the MPI. I pre-set 15 degrees of drift and
started synchronizing, but as I got further along the run I had to
bank out more drift until I had 29 degrees set in. This xx put the
course hair along the metal strip of the nose and I was blacked out
as far as the course went. The rate was killed by using a road that
was adjacent to the target area. Dropped my bombs when ....
. . . .

<<Page 2>>>

2 Narrative

Photographs show visible bomb bursts from 100th "A" Squadron from 750 to 1500 yards NE of MPI. Poor bombing results.

Photographs show visible bursts from 3 A/C from 100 "B" Squadron to be 500 yards SSW of MPI. Poor bombing results.

Photographs of 100th "C" Squadron show visible bomb bursts 500 yards NNW of MPI. Poor bombing results.

100th Bomb Group was the 7th in the Third Division column. Bombers were on a Mag heading of from 320 to 325 when the E/A made their attacks from 5 to 7 oclock high. The formation was good and tightened up when bandits were reported. however, there were stragglers due to flak over the target. The E/A attacked near the R.P., as the Group was forming and made attacks from 1155 hours to 1210 hours and from 5320N-0930E to 5330N-0910E. Formations were at approximately 22,000 feet altitude. Crews believed their escort was engaged in dog fights several miles distant while the E/A pressed their attacks. There were mainly FW 190's with avery few ME 109's and jet propelled ME 262's with a total of 50 E/A in the various attacks which were made by single E/A or in pairs. Most of the E/A pilots seemed to be very skilled. A few seemed fairly green. There was nothing unusual about the enemy's armament or equipment. Most of their A/C were silver with red and black markings. A few had grey fuselages and yellow tails and a few were painted with a yellowish brown camouflage paint. All three squadrons and the composite squadron were attacked. Nearly all passes came from high rear from the E/A passing through the bomber formation or breaking off short and diving below. Then they came in again, making pursuit curves and came in from high rear. Severa B-17's were seen going down smoking and flaming.

-Flak: Frisian Islands: Meager, distant.
Heligoland: Meager, distant.
Bransbuttelkoog: Meager, pointed, inaccurate.
Hamburg: Intense-barrage and tracking. Usually large bursts and accurate.
Wessermunde: Moderate, tracking, accurate.
Nearly all flak damage came immediately after bombsway.

-Weather was 6 to 8/10 middle clouds on route in and back but CAVU over target.

All squadrons and three A/C of the composite squadron encountered E/A and the fighter escort was nil during the attacks. Fighter escorts made rendesvous but were out of sight from shortly thereafter till after the E/A attacks. Then four P-51's and four P-47's were seen.

100th "A" Squadron lost 3 A/C, one due to E/A and two due to a collision resulting from one A/C being hit by flak.

100th "B" Squadron lost 4 A/C, three due to E/A and one due to a combination of E/A and flak.

100th "C" Squadron lost four A/C, two to E/A and two as a result of a collision in which one rode the other pick-a-back to the ground.

31 Dec. 1944

<<Page 3>>

117

handwritten: LT GLENN ROJOHN - 350 - 21 DEC 44 HAMBURG POW MISSION # 241

LT GLENN ROJOHN

MEMO   LT GLENN ROJOHN

LT GLENN ROJOHN; PIGGY BACK LANDING AFTER THE 31 DEC 1944 HAMBURG MISSION. COLLISION WITH LT MacNAB WHILE BOTH WERE ATTEMPTING TO FILL THE SLOT IN THE FORMATION CAUSED BY THE LOSS OF LT WEBSTER. ACCOUNT GIVEN IN "CENTURY BOMBER" FOLLOWS:

AT 1244 HOURS AND AFTER LEAVING THE ENEMY COAST, NAVIGATOR DANNY SHAFFER, WHO FLEW WITH THOMAS HUGHES, NOTED IN HIS LOG: "TWO 17'S HOOKED TOGETHER, 43-31987, PILOTED BY GLENN ROJOHN, HAVING CLOSED UP INTO THE SPACE LEFT BY THE LOSS OF LT WEBSTER. UNFORTUNATELY B-17 43-38457, PILOTED BY WILLIAM MacNAB, HAD RISEN SLOWLY FROM BELOW TO FILL THE SAME POSITION.."

ANOTHER PILOT, ETHAN PORTER, WHO IS LISTED AS HAVING NO KNOWN ADDRESS BY THE VA(1992), IMMEDIATELY SHOUTED A WARNING VIA RADIO, THE TWO FORTRESSES COLLIDED AND LOCKED TOGETHER, CONTINUED FLYING PIGGY-BACK OVER THE SEA.'

FINDING THE ELEVATORS AND AILERONS STILL WORKING, ROJOHN AND HIS CO-PILOT WILLIAM LEEK, 'CUT THIER ENGINES, AND BY USING THE ENGINES OF THE LOWER AIRCRAFT, THREE OF WHICH WERE STILL RUNNING, SLOWLY TURNED THE TWO AIRCRAFT TOWARD LAND. FOUR OF THE CREW BAILED OUT ON ORDERS AND ROJOHN DECENDED TO RECROSS THE ENEMY COAST AT 10,000 FEET. ON LANDING NEAR WILHELMSHAVEN THE TOP SHIP (43-31987) SLID OFF MacNAB'S 43-38457 WHICH EXPLODED. BARELY HURT ROJOHN AND LEEK WALKED AWAY FROM THE WRECKAGE OF 43-31987 AND INTO CAPTIVITY.

AS FOR THE MEN WHO BAILED OUT, THE ROG EDWARD NEUHAUS CAME DOWN ON AN ISLAND; TTE ORVILLE ELKIN CAME DOWN IN THE WATER TEN MILES OFF SHORE AND WAS DRAGGED TO THE SHORE BY HIS CHUTE. REPLACEMENTS NAVIGATOR ROBERT WASHINGTON AND GUNNER JAMES SHRILEY LANDED ON THE COAST. ALL SURVIVORS WERE TAKEN PRISONER. NOTHING WAS FOUND OF BTG JOSEPH RUSSO AND WG FRANCIS CHASE.

AS FOR LT MacNAB--HE WAS KILLED ALONG WITH THE CO-PILOT NELSON VAUGHN (BOTH HAD SUSTAINED WOUNDS PRIOR TO THE COLLISION), ROG HENRY ETHRIDGE, WG DUANE RENCH AND TG FRANCIS SEYFRIED. SGT'S RENCH AND SEYFRIED ARE BOTH BELIEVED TO HAVE BAILED OUT SUCCESSFULLY ONLY TO PERISH IN THE SEA.

THE REST ESCAPED THE AIRCRAFT AND BECAME POWS: NAVIGATOR JACK BERKOWITZ AND BOMBARDIER RAYMOND COMER. FROM THE HONG KONG WILSON CREW, TTE JOSEPH CHADWICK AND BTG EDWARD WOODALL. SGTS WOODALL AND CHADWICK ALSO LANDED IN THE SEA BUT REACHED SHORE.

JIM BROWN NOTES THAT PREVIOUS TO THIS WHEN THE CREW COMPONENT WAS REDUCED TO NINE, WG LENO DELMOLINO WAS ASSIGNED TO INTELLEGENCE IN THE 351ST.

Memo on Lt. Glenn Rojohn 350 Squadron 31 Dec 44 Hamburg Mission #241

LOG BOOK

December 31, 1944 10.34 to 13.10		North Navy Command. Situation Attention Alert. FLAK alert heavy bomber alert with heavy fighter pro-section with continual coming and going to the northern part of the island, direction to the east. In the east Fortress and Mustangs. The formation stayed out of our FLAK range.
	Wind 6-7 from North Clouds 6-10 Visibility 44 kms. Temperature +1.5 Cent.	
10.45		North of LANGEOOG 2 bombs in in the water.
10.56 - 13.00		Radio system extremely disturbed. No measurements possible; partly impossible.
11.24		3 bombs in northeast
11.45 to 13.03		EA's flying back from SE through the section north to W and NW.
12.13 to 12.59		Shooting at the formation and on single flying EA's which probably were already hit. Planes with 13 FLAK guns direct targeting in N and NE target altitude 9000-1800 feet. 408 shots.
12.47		2 Fortress collided in a formation in the NE. The planes flew hooked together and flew 20 miles S. Approximately 10 crew members bailed out one after the other. One man landed on WANGEROOG and put in custody. The rest of enemies were pushed by the wind against the mainland. The two planes were unable to fight anymore The crash could be awaited so I stopped the firing at these 2 planes. 3 rounds of destructive firing on single home flying Fortresses. The same plane shot down from WANGEROOGE by precise gunnery.
Signed by:	DINKELACKER Commanding Officer of the AA Wangerooge	Important observance: formations and fighter groups on the way to Hamburg out of our reach. On the flight back were in scattered forma-tion. Mostly single planes returning.

DINKELACKER (Commanding Officer of the AA Wangerooge Log Book entry for December 31, 1944

Drawing by Bruno Albers of the Operation Center when the collision was spotted

Drawing by Bruno Albers of flak manufacturing building

3542-22nd Avenue
Kenosha, Wi. 53140
Oct. 16, 97

,I'm writing to provide you with my knowledge of the December 31, 1944 air raid over Hamburg.

I flew on Harold Bucklew's crew, on the Silver Dollar, in the ball turret operator's position. My first sighting of an enemy aircraft occurred, I believe, while on the bomb run. An FW 190 was being pursued by a P-51 and they flew past us at about fifty feet to our left. A few seconds later, I saw debris of the FW falling past us. Looking behind and, to the right of our aircraft, I saw two B-17's flying together in formation and each had one engine on fire. After a few seconds, they separated from each other. They were about four hundred feet apart and flying parallel with each other for a few minutes, when they both exploded almost simultaneously. I then looked below to the right of my aircraft, where I saw FW 190's making their attacks on a formation of B-17's. One of the FW's, after making his pass at this squadron, turned upward and started to approach my aircraft. I had him framed perfectly in my reticles and fired at him when he came into range. The FW disappeared in a puff of black smoke and I called on the intercom that I got the FW. I thought it exploded but a few seconds later, most of the smoke cleared and he was still there, only now a small amount of smoke was coming from his engine. The FW pilot put the nose of his plane down and headed away in a shallow glide. I watched him until he got out of sight. I'm sure he turned away because he received some damage. The next thing that I noticed was a lot of fighter planes falling in flames about a mile behind us. I couldn't see above where the dog fights were taking place, but I did see the fighters falling almost like rain. I could hardly believe my eyes! This went on for some time. The planes stopp-

Letter from Paul Zak from Harold Bucklew Crew 2 page document

ed falling after awhile, but a few seconds later I saw another bunch of planes coming down, it seemed like all at one time. The falling then slowed up and stopped. I remember that at the time, it reminded me of a bunch of burning matchsticks coming down. After leaving the target area, we found ourselves flying alone toward the North Sea. To our left, was McNabb's B-17 flying alone toward the coast and to the left of him and behind was Glenn Rojohn's plane. A few minutes later, Rojohn's plane passed over the top of McNabb's; they touched and stuck together. They were flying as one plane, an unbelievable sight! Smoke was pouring out of one of Rojohn's right engines and the two planes stuck together, began making a large circle turn to the left. I called our navigator, to give him the tail numbers of both aircraft. I also counted the chutes that came from both planes. All this time, the two planes kept making a large circle to the left. Although we were flying away from them, I could see that the circles kept moving them toward land. I saw a German patrol boat heading in the direction of some of the chutes coming down. I watched the two planes locked together until they disappeared from my vision.

At the Long Beach Reunion, I met and talked to Rojohn and his crew, along with some members of McNabb's crew, about the Piggyback Ride over Hamburg. I told them that I was the one that got their tail numbers and this information was given at the debriefing.

Sincerely,

Paul Zak
100th Bomb Group
418th Squadron

Paul Zack letter p. 2

Dec. 31 st., New Year's Eve coming up. The day started out as usual, went to navigator's pre briefing + was told the target was Hamburg + we proceded as usual.

The first half of the mission was uneventful + normal. Our problems started when we turned North at the initial point + started ~~down the~~ BACK FROM THE target. The wind was very strong + slowed the planes down to almost a walk. It was a clear day + the 88's coming from the ground were giving us trouble. At that time we were attacked by ME 109's + FW 190's + a few jet fighters. We tried to get over the North Sea because the enemy fighters would not follow us as a rule because of gas shortage. As we were flying

Letter from Jack Berkowitz, Navigator of Nine Lives, Macnab Crew 2 pages

OVER THE COAST, OUR WING MAN WAS HIT & WE TRIED TO FILL THE EMPTY SPOT. AT THE SAME TIME, ANOTHER B-17 PILOTED BY LT. LOJOHN ALSO WENT FOR THE SAME SPOT & SETTLED ON TOP OF OUR PLANE & IT LOOKED LIKE WE HAD AN 8 ENGINE BOMBER.

LTS. McHALE & VAUGHN WERE KILLED A LITTLE EARLIER & I WAS HIT IN THE LEG. LT. COMER, BOMBADIER & I THEN LEFT FROM THE ESCAPE HATCH IN THE NOSE OF THE PLANE. WE WERE OVER THE NORTH SEA WHEN WE JUMPED & FREE FELL TO GET BELOW THE FIGHTING. LUCKILY, THE WIND WAS IN OUR FAVOR & IT TOOK US ONTO THE BEACH. IN THE MEANTIME, THE GERMANS HAD TAKEN PICTURES OF WHAT SEEMED TO BE AN 8 ENGINE BOMBER, AND I WAS SHIPPED TO AN INTERROGATION CENTER IN FRANKFORT, GERMANY & PUT INTO

Jack Berkowitz letter p.2

Edward L. Woodall Jr.
1772 Sunview Road
Lyndhurst, Ohio 44124
(216) 442-2945

January 2, 1990

William Kirkpatrick
511 S. E. 18th Avenue
Cape Coral, FL 33990

Re: Rojohn/MacNab Piggy Back Mid-air Collision

Dear Bill:

It was a pleasure to meet and talk with you at the 100th B.G. Reunion in Tampa this past November.

I am enclosing copies of the Operational Narrative for the 31 December 1944 Mission and the Individual Casualty Questionaires completed by the surviving members of our crew after we were returned to the United States. The microfilms weren't too clear, as you can see from the enlarged copies of the Casualty Questionaires. I am indebted to Leo Ross for taking time to redo the Operational Narrative.

This was our 22nd Mission.

I was the ball turret gunner on MacNab's crew assigned to AC 43-38457. We were lead for the high flight of the low "C" Squadron. Our wing men were AC 43-38409 piloted by Leo Ross, and AC 43-38436 Piloted by Charles Webster. I do not know where Rojohn was flying in the formation.

Following the bomb drop, we were attacked by fighters near the R. P. and lost Webster, followed by Ross. As a result, we were flying alone as far as our flight was concerned. By this time the formation was up over the East Frisian Islands in the North Sea. A crew check was called and all reported in okay just prior to the mid-air collision.

At the time of the impact, we lost all power and intercom on our aircraft. I knew we were in trouble from the violent shaking of the aircraft. no power to operate the turret, loss of intercom, and seeing falling pieces of metal. My turret was stalled with the guns up at about 9 o'clock. This is where countless time drills covering emergency escape procedures from the turret paid off, as I automatically reached for the hand crank, disengaged the clutch and proceeded to crank the turret and guns to the down position so I could open the door and climb into the waist of the airplane. I do not remember disconnecting my oxygen mask, intercom and heated suit connections.

Letter from Ed Woodall, Ball Turret Gunner of Nine Lives, Macnab Crew 3 pages

Edward L. Woodall Jr.
1772 Sunview Road
Lyndhurst, Ohio 44124
(216) 442-2945

2.......

After getting out of the turret, I looked for other E.M. crew
members in the back of the aircraft and saw Sgt. Ethridge
sitting in the rear door preparing to bail out. At that point, I
was the only one left in that area of the aircraft as Sgts. Rench
and Seyfried had already bailed out. I could see that another
aircraft was locked onto our aircraft with his props buried in
our wings and his ball turret jammed down inside our aircraft.

I finally located my parachute and bailed out. Contrary to the
report in Richard L. Strange's "CENTURY BOMBERS" I did not come
down in the sea but made a very poor landing on the beach and
was dragged inland by a very strong gale-like wind. As a result
of my 'crash' landing, I suffered broken bones in my right foot
and a fracture of the right hip and pelvic bone which made it
impossible for me to collapse my chute, and I was finally stopped
when it became entangled in a fence.

I was immediately picked up by the home guard and taken to a
small village and held there the remainder of the afternoon while
the rest of the survivors were gradually brought in. Later in
the day we were all taken to a Luftwaffe Base.

The aircraft crashed at, or near Tittens, Germany.

There were ten (10) survivors from this accident; six (6) from
Rojohn's crew and four (4) from MacNab's crew. I am listing the
rest from my crew who might be willing to give you much more
information as to what happened up front on our plane prior to
the collision.

· ¬¬⁺or)

572-2714

Four of my crew who we_____   ion
are either buried or listed on _____   the
Netherlands Cemetary, Margraten, Netherlands. They ar~

Ed Woodall letter p. 2

Edward L. Woodall Jr.
1772 Sunview Road
Lyndhurst, Ohio 44124
(216) 442-2945

3.....

Lt. MacNab and Sgts. Ethridge, Rench and Seyfried.

Lt. Vaughn's remains were returned to the United States and are buried in the Lincoln Memorial Park, Portland, Oregon in 1949.

I wish I could give you more information as to exactly what took place prior to and during the collision between the two aircraft on that fateful day, but my position on the crew prevented any eyewitness account of what actually occured.

Good luck in your search for more concrete facts for your article on our tragic accident on 31 December 1944. If you think of anything else I might help you with, please do not hesitate to contact me.

Sincerely,

Ed Woodall, Jr.

Edward L. Woodall, Jr.

Encls:

Ed Woodall letter p.3

The 100th Bomb Group Mission to Hamburg
New Year's Eve December 31, 1944

by G. A. Fuller

Set forth in this paper is a simplistic version of the 100th Bomb Group mission to Hamburg, Germany, on December 31, 1944, New Year's Eve. It is prepared primarily for background information for the portrayal of the mission painted by Robert Bailey for the Omaha Reunion. It is also hoped it will bring discussion of the mission by the survivors.

The 100th Bomb Group led the 13th Combat Wing on this mission. Don Jones was the lead pilot of the lead squadron. Charles Martin was the command pilot, Art Juhlin, lead navigator, Storm Rhode, the radar operator, and Tom Barrett, lead bombardier. Charles "Hong Kong" Wilson was the lead pilot and Harry Cruver the command pilot of the high squadron (deputy lead) and Jean DePlanque the lead pilot and Ed Wooten, the command pilot of the low squadron. I was Don Jones co-pilot and flew in the tail of the lead ship.

Following this page is a schedule showing the formation positions of those crews on the mission.

Grant Fuller, witness, 2 page documentation

Our formation left the English coast without problems. Hamburg is only 60 to 70 miles north of East Anglia so our route was basically eastward over the North Sea. Flying over the North Sea was preferable inasmuch as there was no flak and the German fighters did not fly out for battle because they were no more interested in coming down in the North Sea than we were. We always understood you had about 40 seconds to escape the freezing waters. We had an unusually strong tail wind of about 140 mi/hr, but more on that later.

No one seems to remember the identity of the IP (initial point of the bomb run) but it is recalled that we were careful to not violate the airspace of Denmark, so the IP was near Denmark. That meant our bomb run to Hamburg was north to south. The direction of the run required a near 90-degree right turn against a 140-mi/hr wind. After the turn, the 140-mi/hr wind became a cross wind. Tom Barrett states the maximum turn you could make with the bomb sight was 45 degrees. He had it all cranked in and was still moving off the target. He finally released the bombs by eyeing the target.

The extensive turns of the lead squadron caused big problems for the high and low squadrons. The high squadron was on the inside of the turns and, with the strong crosswind, could not hold its position and had to make a large S turn out and back. This left a gap after the lead squadron. Hong Kong Wilson, very aware of the gap advised Wooten and DePlanque in the low to follow the lead squadron over the target. The high squadron then was last over the target.

- 1 -

Grant Fuller witness statement p.2

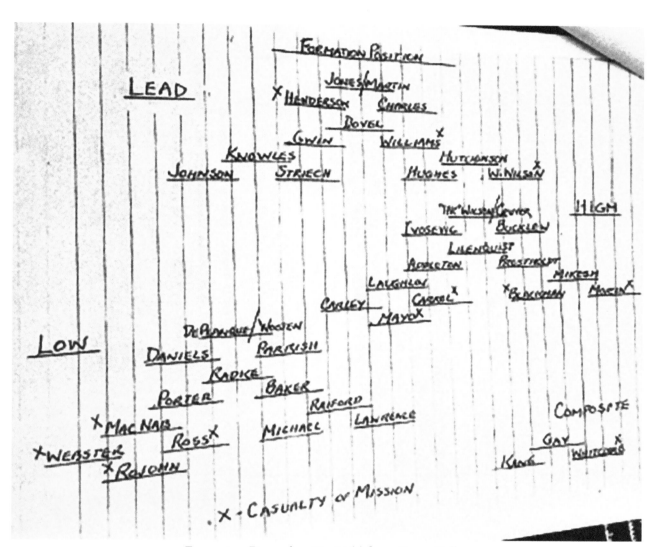

Formation December 31, 1944 from Grant Fuller

S P L A S H E R   S I X

THE NEWSLETTER OF THE 100TH BOMB GROUP ASSOCIATION

Harry H. Crosby, Editor
Smart's Hill Farm - Lovell, Maine 04051

207/925-2431

Monday, August 21, 1989

Mr. Bill Kilpatrick
511 SE 18th Avenue
Cape Coral, Florida 33904

                    c: Glenn Rojohn

Dear Bill:

    Here is another source for information about the Piggy-back Saga, from:

            George Rubin
            11421 Nark's Drive
            Conifir, Colorado 80433

            303/838-950?

    As I understand it, George was the radio operator, flying with Raiford as pilot, on the mission when the two planes collided. George tells the story very graphically. He remembers that we lost twelve planes on that day with some of the worst dogfights he ever saw.

    Rojohn and McNabb were great, he says. When the squadron's lead plane, with Bob Rosenthal at pilot and Dave Lyster as command, got into trouble and had to drop back, McNabb had to take over. In the exchange, the two planes collided, smoothly, a perfect fit, Rojohn's plane from the bottom and McNabb's from the top. There were sparks, and george was very frightened, but the two planes stayed together. It happen just off the Raiford/Rubin right wing.

    George says that although the mission was more than forty years ago, he remembers it like yesterday. He may be useful for color and detail.

    I will send a copy of this letter to Glenn Rojohn for confirmation. I hope all goes well.

Yours.

1

Letter from George Rubin, witness

Badger S Dak
St Pats day 17

Dear Cindi

I swear on Dec 31-1944 We
(MIKESH CREW) were Fireball able
High.

We lost John Morris crew on our left
wing and Bill Blackemans crew on
our left.

"Mik" was flying at the time so I had
full vision of Rojohns crew forming on our
right wing when I saw McNabs plane pull
up under Rojohns plane —

Negative dihedral stopped them from
separation so Rojohn took both back
to land at Germany rather than the
north Sea — Happy new year.

Ralph Christensen

Letter from Ralph Christensen, witness

133

These are my recallections of Dec. 31, 1944.

We turned south off the North Sea and headed for Hamburg. The target and the sky over it were black from miles away. The flak was brutal. We flew through flak clouds and aircraft parts for what seemed like an hour. When we passed the flak we turned west. One of the crew said, he was glad to see our fighter escort at last. Above us was a cluster of circling con-trails. I remembered that our "little friends" flew parallel to us about 1000 feet higher. They only circled during a fight. We turned North. Over the inter-com I heard a yell that these B__ _ _s were shooting at us. He was right.

I had been at the controls when we came off the bomb run. Glenn and I alternated the controls each half hour so that the man resting could enjoy the view. On this mission the lead plane was off Glenn's wing, so he flew the bomb run. I should have kept the controls for at least my half-hour, but once the attack began, our formation tight-ened up and we started bouncing up and down. Our lead plane kept go-ing out of sight for me. I may have been over-correcting, but the planes all seemed to bounce at different times. I asked Glenn to take it and he did.

In the cockpit we could hear our fifties firing and I think Russo yelled that he had a sure hit.. I'd forgotten that our guns could be "felt" as well as heard. They felt good. A FW190 went by close to my wing and I remember thinking that it could use a paint job. Two others joined it and they peeled off to the right for another pass. This was a long trip. When we finally reached the North Sea we turned west back to England. I am sure that we were still under attack. We always called for a condition check to each position when we got into the clear. We did not call that day.

We had not been on a Westerly course very long when our lives were ab-ruptly changed. I think that the other B17 came up under us, because we lunged upward. The two planes ground together like breeding Dragon-flies. Glenn's outboard prop bent into the nacel of the lower plane's engine. Glenn gunned our engines two or three times to try to fly us off. It didn't work, but it was a good try. The outboard left engine was burning on the plane below. We feathered our propellers and rang the bail-out bell.

The two planes would drop into a dive unless we pulled back all the time. Glenn pointed left and we turned the mess toward land. I felt Elkin touch my shoulder and waived him back through the bomb bay. We got over land and Shirley came up from below. I signalled to him to follow Elkin. Finally Bob Washington came up from the nose. He was just hanging on between our seats. Glenn waived him back with the others. We were dropping fast.

Letter from Bill Leek, Co-Pilot- 2pages

-2-

I could hear Russo saying his Hail Mary's over the inter-com. I could not help him and I felt that I was somehow invading his right to be alone. I pulled off my helmet and noticed that we were at 15,000 feet. This was the hardest part of the ride for me.

Awhile later, we were shot at by guns that made a round white puff like big dandilion seeds ready to be blown away. By now the fire was pouring over our left wing and I wondered just what those German gunners thought we were up to and where we were going! Before long fifty caliber shells began to blow at random in the plane below. I don't know if the last flak had started more or if the fire had spread, but it was hot down there!

We just had to hang on. Glenn had told me to follow Bob and bail out, but I refused. I was sure that a man who was 24 years old was not strong enough to hold these planes level while I went through the bomb bay to the waist door, and if they had gone into a spin, escape would not be possible. And - one man left in the wreck could not have survived, so I stayed to go along for the ride.

At one point I tried to beat my way out of the window with a veripistol. I still don't know why--just panic. The ground came up faster and faster. Praying was allowed. We had our feet on the instrument panel for more leverage. Glenn seemed frozen in one position. I hit him on the shoulder and screamed -"Pull!" We gave it one last effort and slammed into the ground.

We slid off the other plane and seemed to pound the earth at intervals until we came to a stop. When my adrenalin began to lower I looked around, Glenn was OK- I was OK and a convenient hole was available for a fast exit. It was a break just behind the cockpit. I crawled out onto the left wing to wait for Glenn. I pulled out a cigarette and was about to light it when a young German soldier with a rifle came slowly up to the wing, making me keep my hands up. He grabbed the cigarette out of my mouth and pointed down. The wing was covered with gasoline. Glenn soon came out, we got down and learned that for us, "The war was over".

Bill Leek

Bill Leek statement p.2

CHAPTER 6

LIFE AS A PRISONER OF WAR

The excitement of the crash landing was abruptly stopped by an influx of German officials. Word was spread "THE AMERICANS" have a new 8 engine super plane. The Germans wanted answers.

And the citizens wanted to participate on a scavenger hunt. German witness Fran Hinrichs (13 years old at the time) described the scene, "Some of the women tried to get hold of the soldiers' chute to make a blouse out of it. My brother shouted 'The chute stays with the men.' He went to the landing spot and found some C-rations, goodies, and chewing gum. We were very happy." Also mentioned was taking a soldier into the house for a cup of tea.

They landed in an area in Germany that saw few confrontations with the United States. They did not have facilities to deal with all these men falling from the sky. Lts. Rojohn and Leek were whisked away for interrogation as German officials were racing to get there from all directions. What happened during that in interrogation is a mystery since that was an aspect of the incident Glenn Rojohn didn't talk about. When asked a question about interrogation and imprisonment during a speech in Pleasant Hills, PA he got still and somber. Part of his answer was "I was surprised that they knew EVERYTHING about me. They knew rank, serial number, social security number, my commander's name, how many missions I flew, when I was born and my parent's name."

When German officials were notified by witnesses that a collision of two planes happened in midair, there was no need to continue interrogation about a super plane. The officials had no more use for Lts. Rojohn and Leek at this time so they were released from their custody to the Germans who were waiting outside. Glenn and Bill were put into trucks to pick up the rest of the crew members. No one spoke in fear of repercussion. Both Rojohn and Washington reported locking eyes with each other and feeling great happiness both had survived. Rojohn and Washington became friends in war and remained life long friends.

The surviving members of The Little Skipper and Nine Lives were put together in a room. German citizen, Wilma Tepe, identified it as GASTHOUS LANGMARK which was an Inn. Jack Berkowitz, navigator from Nine Lives, fainted when he heard the orders of one of the German official. He told everyone later that what he heard was "If they move, shoot them." Jack was the only one in the group who spoke German. The crew members were divided up and loaded into different vehicles to be processed. Then some were transported to Stalag Luft III. Washington, Berkowitz, and Comer were sent to Stalag Luft I. Rojohn and Leek were transported to a facility in Frankfort to be placed in solitary confinement for interrogation purposes for two weeks. They were then transported to Stalag Luft I. Glenn H Rojohn's home at Stalag Luft I was North 3 Barracks 9 Block 309 Room 2.

Even though Glenn H. Rojohn talked about his legendary, historical mid air collision, he never spoke of his POW experience other than he never wanted to see or eat a rutabaga ever again. After we discovered his collection, we learned from his Short Snorter (a money bill signed by himself and those in camp with him) that Washington, Leek and Comer were with him. At the end of the speech in Pleasant Hills, PA, he was asked how he was treated as a POW. His very quiet answer was "They followed the rules of the Geneva Convention."

Documents in Chapter 6

1. Cover of Lt. Glenn Rojohn's POW Diary
2. What was included in Glenn H. Rojohn's Diary
3. Items in An American Red Cross Diary
4. Activities in Kriegie Camp
5. Personal Notes from Glenn H. Rojohn's POW Diary
6. Telegram taken POW
7. POW Record, front page
8. Post Card Dulag Luft
9. Map of POW camps
10. Information about Stalag Luft I
11. POW Camp set up
12. Short Snorted both sides
13. Chaplin letter sent to families
14. 1/18/45 Letter sent from POW Camp
15. Letter from Mrs. Rojohn to Mrs. Leek
16. Post Card from POW Camp 1/28/45
17. MIA Telegram
18. Letter from Mrs. Rojohn to Mrs. Leek about plane down
19. Notification from War Department MIA
20. Telegram from War Department POW
21. Newspaper clipping Glenn POW, Leonard completed missions
22. Post Card from Shortwave Radio Operator "I'm OK" "Call Jane"
23. Propaganda telegram "I'm OK"
24. Letter 3/10/45 from Stalag Luft I
25. Letter about how to communicate to a POW
26. March 19, 1945 letter from Stalag Luft I
27. March 28, 1945 letter from Stalag Luft I
28. Swastika souvenir taken from.Stalag Luft I

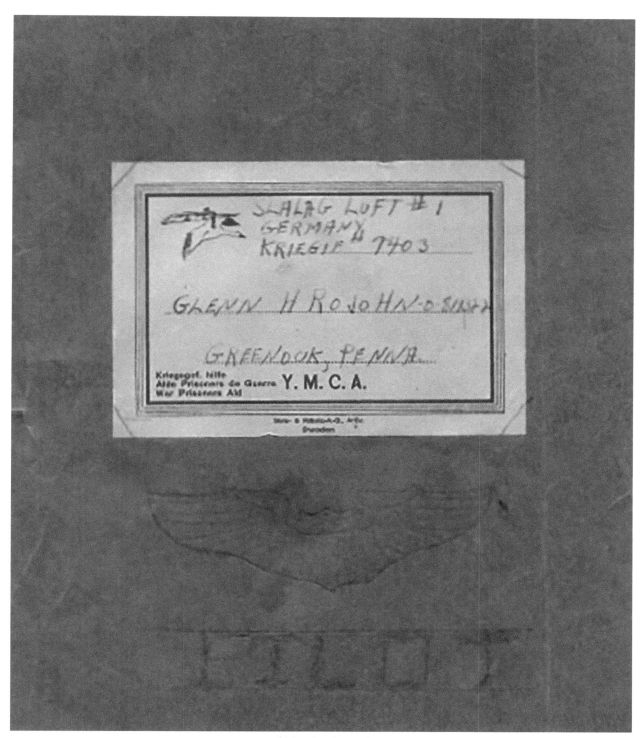

Picture of blue book used as diary

Included in Glenn H. Rojohn's POW Diary
The diary was written in pencil so was not dark enough to copy.

Addresses of those in the camp including Leek, Washington, Neuhaus, Elkin, Berkowitz.
Food the guys talked about that he wanted his mother to make for him to try. Kuchen and graham cracker pudding became his children's favorite.
Places to eat and places to visit in the good old United States.
Items in the American Red Cross Parcel, see next page.
A Days Activities in Kriegie Camp, included.
Glenn H Rojohn's drawing of his room.
List of his crew with addresses.
Things to trade with others with a note of what he needed to get from home to trade.
In addition Glenn H. Rojohn added a few notes not necessarily on continuous days and for a short duration. Some notations were difficult to read after deterioration.

ITEMS IN AN AMERICAN RED CROSS PARCEL

Can of SPAM
Can of corned beef
Box of sugar
5 packs of cigarettes
Can of margarine
Soap
Can of jam
Can of cheese
Box prunes or raisins
Can of meat
Can of vegetable stew
Can of salmon or sardines
Vitamins
Crackers or cereal
Bar of chocolate
Can of coffee
Powered milk
Liver or chicken pate

Lt. Rojohn noted "We are supposed to get 1 parcel per man per week, but that didn't happen once since I have been here. It went down to ¼ parcel per man and then down to none at all. It is quite a treat to see American food."

A DAY'S ACTIVITIES IN KRIEGIE CAMP
(ACCORDING TO Glenn H Rojohn's diary)

Rise at 8 o'clock in time for morning role call.

Go out to parade grounds and be counted by the Germans and exercise.

Breakfast then sit around or take a walk until lunchtime.

After lunch play cards or read.

At four another roll call and more exercises.
Can't put any strength in the exercises because you don't have any.

Patiently wait for supplies which sometimes is only bread and water.

If lights on in the evening which is seldom we play cards.

Usually one fellow gives some kinda talk before hitting the sack.

Bedtime is about 9-9:30 and you put in a night of turning and twisting on your bed of boards and straw.

PERSONAL NOTES FROM GLENN H. ROJOHN'S POW DIARY

Wager about the war's end between Ross, Currie, and GHR--Spend the day together in NYC. Winner gets free all day other 2 have to pay.
Ross -- April 24, 1945
Currie – April 26, 1945
GHR – May 15, 1945

March 23, 1945

Springtime came to Kriegieland. Spent the day outside sunning. Felt good to get some sunshine. Few guys who had the strength playing softball.
"I guess when men get hungry as we are they think of everything."

March 25, 1945

News Montgomery was across the Rhine.
Palm Sunday Sermons every Sunday. "Hope this weather continues. If it does we may be home soon."

March 26, 1945

"I think the end will not be too far off."

March 27, 1945

Dream of home. "¼ Red Cross parcel with chocolate so morals high"
Referring to chewing a Spamburger – I think everyone has learned to appreciate little things that they never did before." Author note—Periodically throughout his life I remember him asking my mother he wanted her to get Spam at the grocery store.

POW DOCUMENTS

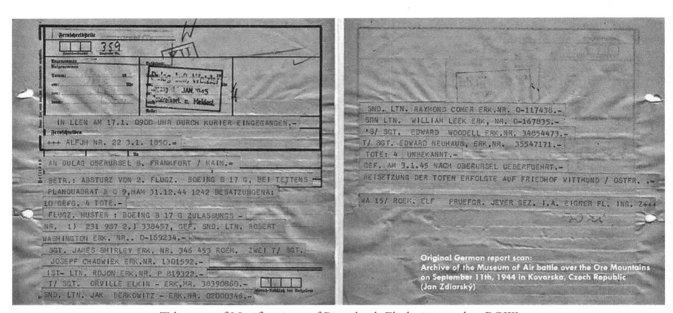

Telegram of Notifications of Piggyback Flight interred as POW

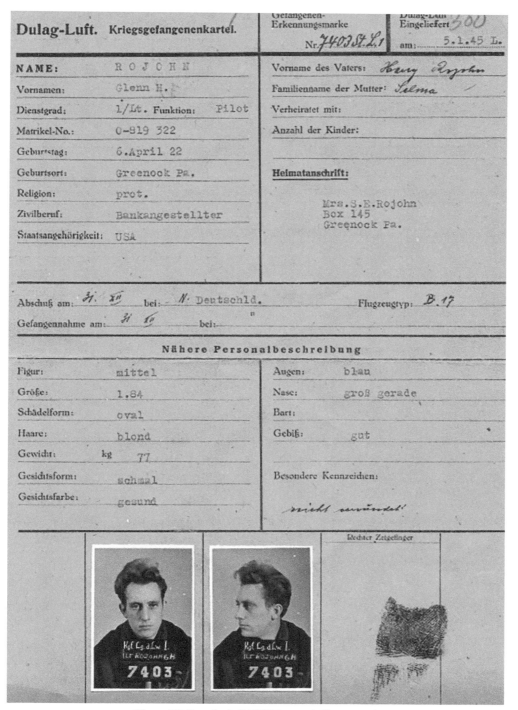

Glenn H Rojohn's POW Record (first page)

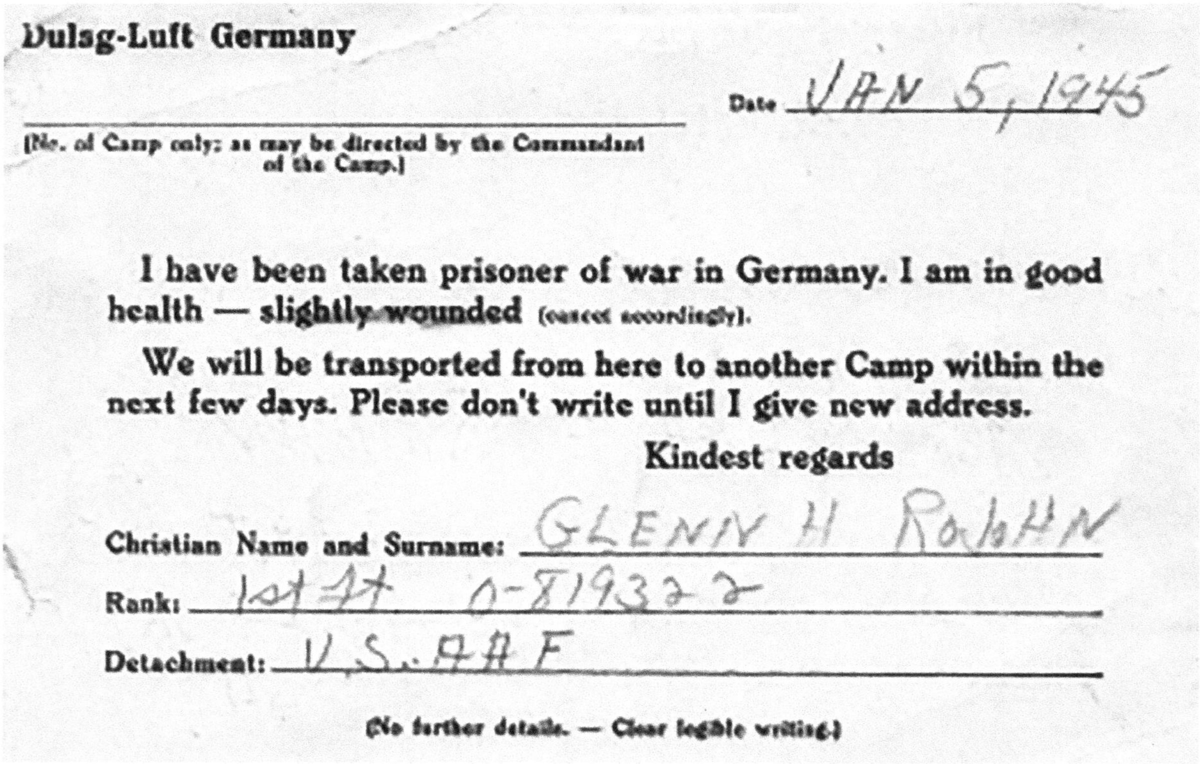

Dulag-Luft Germany

Date JAN 5, 1945

(No. of Camp only; as may be directed by the Commandant of the Camp.)

I have been taken prisoner of war in Germany. I am in good health — ~~slightly wounded~~ (cancel accordingly).

We will be transported from here to another Camp within the next few days. Please don't write until I give new address.

Kindest regards

Christian Name and Surname: GLENN H ROJOHN

Rank: 1st Lt 0-819322

Detachment: U.S. AAF

(No further details. — Clear legible writing.)

Postcard from Dalag-Luft reporting taken POW

Maps of German POW Camps

STALAG LUFT 1, Page 1 of 6

AMERICAN PRISONERS OF WAR IN GERMANY
Prepared by MILITARY INTELLIGENCE SERVICE, WAR DEPARTMENT 15 JULY 1944

STALAG LUFT 1

STRENGTH: 2,867 AAF officers. Several hundred RAF officers and NCOs are also prisoners in this camp.

LOCATION: Pinpoint 54°22' North Latitude, 12°42'30" East Longitude. Camp is situated at Barth, a small town on the Baltic Sea, 23 kilometers Northwest of Stralsund.

DESCRIPTION: Stalag Luft 1 consists of 3 compounds each encircled by barbed wire. Barracks house 120 men apiece. Some of the buildings are divided into small rooms holding from 4 to 10 double-decker bunks, while others are partitioned into larger sections holding 24 two-tier beds. Rooms are well-lighted and adequately ventilated. Heating is generally satisfactory. Every prisoner received a straw mattress and 3 blankets, 2 from the Germans and one from the Red Cross.

TREATMENT: Correct.

FOOD: German rations of potatoes, turnips, bread, and cabbage are inadequate for sustenance. Prisoners live on the food parcels sent by the American, British, and Canadian Red Cross. In 2 of the 3 compounds the occupants of a room usually cook their food and take turns cooking, using forced-draft blowers which they have made from tin cans. In the third and newest compound a communal mess hall is in operation. Small vegetable gardens tilled by the prisoners furnish minute amounts of lettuce, radishes, beets, onions and tomatoes.

CLOTHING: Prisoners are reasonably well clothed and shod. Clothing supplies have come from the Red Cross because of the failure of the Germans to provide them.

HEALTH: Health is excellent. Two British doctors ably minister to the sick in the 20-bed camp infirmary. Patients whose condition require more extensive treatment are taken to a hospital in Neubrandenburg. A civilian dentist visits the camp weekly and is sometimes available in the town for emergency purposes. A full-time dentist, however, is needed. Calisthenics at the Senior American Officer's direction are compulsory twice a week. Showers are provided once a week.

RELIGION: Religious services are conducted in a special building set aside as a chapel. Rev. J. Hall is the Catholic and Rev. B. Drake Brockman the Protestant chaplain. Both are British.

PERSONNEL: American Senior Officer Colonel J.R. Byerly   German Commandant: Oberst Scherer

MAIL: Both surface and airmail from the United States take 4 to 6 months in transit. Average travel time for mail from the camp to this country is 100 days.

RECREATION: POWs play baseball, basketball, football, soccer, softball and volleyball. An organized all-prisoner entertainment program includes frequent performances by the camp orchestra and occasional shows in the theater built by the prisoners. Able PW instructors give course in Music, History, Engineering, Mathematics, Literature, and languages. Books on non-controversial subjects may be drawn from a growing library. Hobbies range from clay sculpturing and casting statuettes out of melted tin foil to embroidery and painting.

WORK: NONE

PAY: NOT KNOWN

General Information about Stalag Luft I

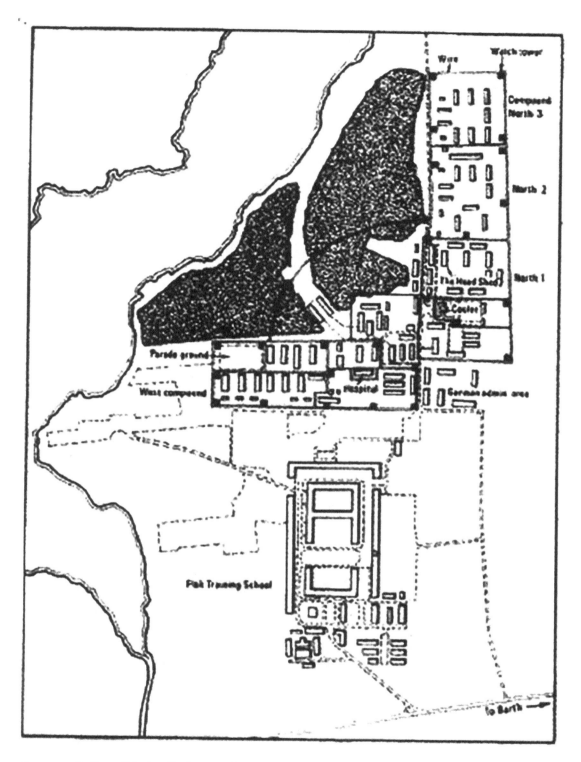

Annotated plan of Stalag Luft I as of January 1945.

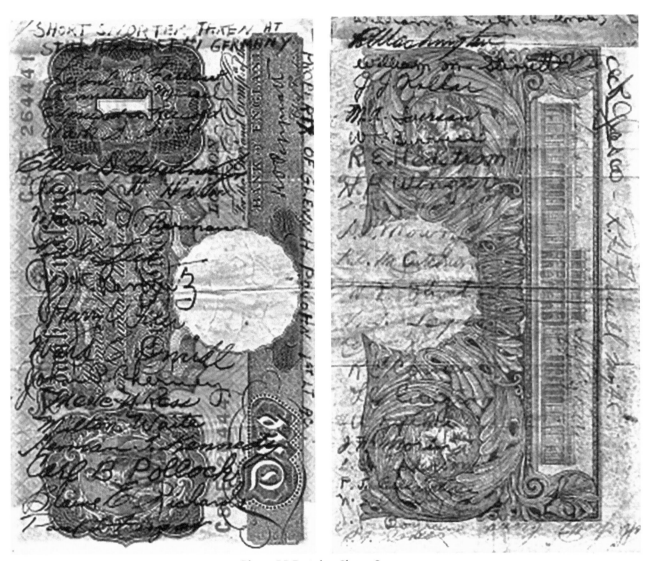

Glenn H Rojohn Short Snorter
Rojohn, Comer, Leek, Washington signatures appear

OFFICE OF THE STATION CHAPLAIN　　　　　　S-A-1
100th Bombardment Group (H)
APO 559, New York, N.Y.

15 January 1945

Mrs. Selma Rojohn,
Box 145,
Greenock, Penna.

Dear Mrs. Rojohn:

Undoubtedly you have received the report from The War Department stating that your son, Glenn H. Rojohn, 1st Lt., ASN O-819322, is missing in action. Pursuant to request from The Commanding General, Eighth Air Force, and in behalf of my Commanding Officer and the men of this station I respectfully extend to you our deepest sympathy in this period of anxiety.

The Casualty Branch of The Adjutant General's Office, War Department, Washington, D. C. will advise you of any change in status as soon as such information can be released. Everything that is known about Glenn and his crew and the mission on which he was reported missing in action has been forwarded to that office and can be released only from that office. I am permitted to release absolutely no information as it would hazard his welfare and that of his friends who are carrying on this task to its completion. Also, our experience has proven that you will hear of any change in his status before we do.

We pray that God may keep your courage high and your faith firm while you await communication from him or about him. The devotion and faithfulness in his unselfish service teach us how we must live. His example can be followed only as we have a strong trust in God who can be with Glenn and you and me - and sustain us all. May you have the comfort and help of The Heavenly Father through all the days ahead.

Sincerely yours,

Glenn F. Teska

GLENN F. TESKA,
Protestant Chaplain.

January 15, 1945 Station of Chaplin Letter Rojohn MIA

1/18/45

DEAR FOLKS: I HOPE BY THIS TIME
YOU ALL HAVE HEARD ABOUT MY MISFORTUNE.
I'LL HAVE ALOT TO TELL YOU ABOUT WHEN
I GET HOME. I HAVE ALREADY RAN INTO
SEVERAL FRIENDS OF MINE. I'M ONLY
ALLOWED TO WRITE THREE LETTERS A MONTH
AND A COUPLE POST CARDS. WRITE TO ME

AS MUCH AS YOU CAN. THE RED CROSS
IS SWELL IN MY OPINION. MAKE THEM A
DONATION OUT OF MY ACCOUNT. GIVE ALL
MY FRIENDS THE NEWS ABOUT ME AND
I'LL SEE THEM IN TIME. IF SOME FRIENDS
FROM THE SOUTH WRITE TELL THEM ALSO.
I HOPE BY THIS T___ ___ ___ THE
LEONARD IS HOME. TELL THE OLD BOY
HELLO. ANY INFORMATION REGARDING MY
PERSONAL BELONGINGS CAN BE OBTAINED
FROM THE RED CROSS. MOM I HOPE YOU ARE
FEELING BETTER. I THINK OF YOU ALL ALOT.
HOPE DAD THAT THE COMPANY IS DOING
FINE. I AM FEELING GOOD AND AND GETTING
ALONG OK. CALL THE BANK AND GIVE
THEM THE NEWS. I SHALL WRITE AGAIN
SOON. UNTIL THEN SO LONG. GLENN.

January 18, 1945 letter from POW camp

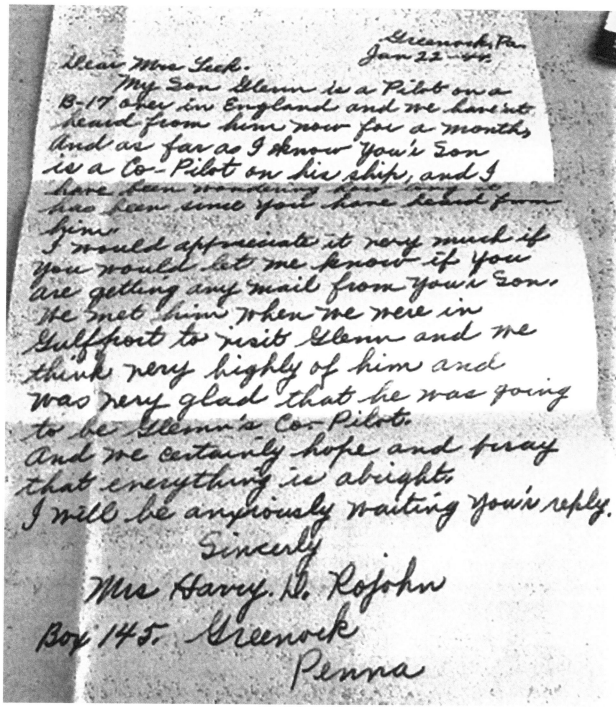

Greenock, Pa.
Jan 22 — 45

Dear Mrs Leek.

My Son Glenn is a Pilot on a B-17 over in England and we have not heard from him now for a month, And as far as I know Your Son is a Co-Pilot on his ship, and I have been wondering how long it has been since you have heard from him

I would appreciate it very much if you would let me know if you are getting any mail from Your Son. We met him when we were in Gulfport to visit Glenn and we think very highly of him and was very glad that he was going to be Glenn's Co-Pilot. And we certainly hope and pray that everything is alright.

I will be anxiously waiting your reply.

Sincerly

Mrs Harry. D. Rojohn
Box 145. Greenock
Penna

Letter January 22 1945 to Bill Leek's mother from Glenn's mother Provided by Kim Leek Catacutan

Kriegsgefangenenlager   Datum: JAN 28, 1945.

DEAR FOLKS: HERE I AM AGAIN. ITS HARD
TO KNOW WHAT TO WRITE BUT TO LET
YOU KNOW I'M OK. WE ARE GETTING
OK SO FAR. BILL IS HERE WITH ME.
SURE HOPE EVERONE IS IN GOOD HEALTH.
ALSO THAT THE BUSINESS IS OK. WRITE BROTHER
AND TELL HIM I'M OK. SOLONG - GLENN.

Postcard from POW Camp written 1/28/45

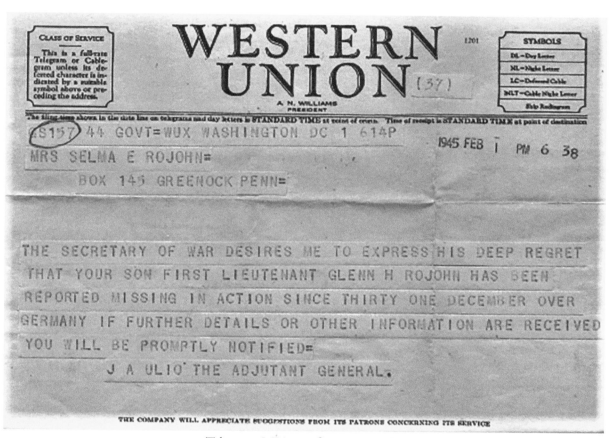

Telegram MIA notification 2/1/45

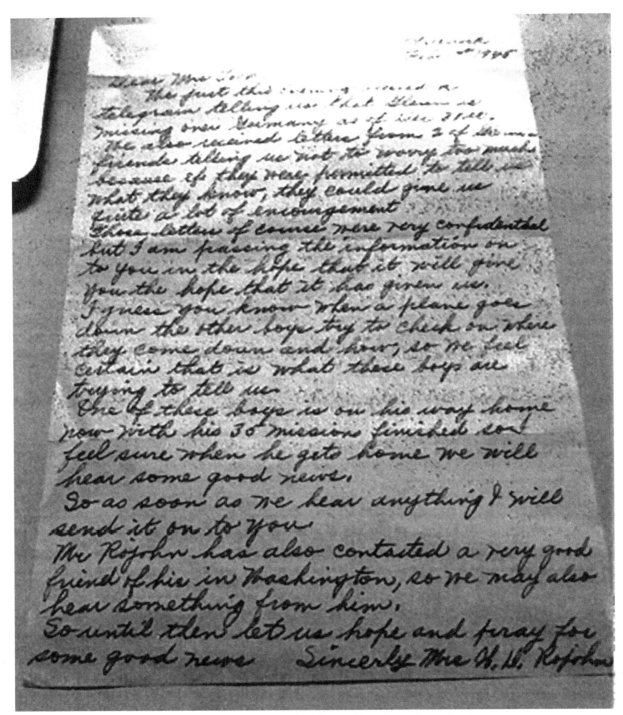

Letter 2/1/45 to Bill Leek's mother from Glenn's mother after learning
the plane went down Provided by Kim Leek Catacutan

WAR DEPARTMENT

THE ADJUTANT GENERAL'S OFFICE

WASHINGTON 25, D. C.

IN REPLY REFER TO:
AG 201 Rojohn, Glenn H.
PC-N ETO 012

2 February 1945

Mrs. Selma E. Rojohn
Box 145
Greenock, Pennsylvania

Dear Mrs. Rojohn:

This letter is to confirm my recent telegram in which you were regretfully informed that your son, First Lieutenant Glenn H. Rojohn, 0819322, has been reported missing in action over Germany since 31 December 1944.

I know that added distress is caused by failure to receive more information or details. Therefore, I wish to assure you that at any time additional information is received it will be transmitted to you without delay, and, if in the meantime no additional information is received, I will again communicate with you at the expiration of three months. Also, it is the policy of the Commanding General of the Army Air Forces upon receipt of the "Missing Air Crew Report" to convey to you any details that might be contained in that report.

The term "missing in action" is used only to indicate that the whereabouts or status of an individual is not immediately known. It is not intended to convey the impression that the case is closed. I wish to emphasize that every effort is exerted continuously to clear up the status of our personnel. Under war conditions this is a difficult task as you must readily realize. Experience has shown that many persons reported missing in action are subsequently reported as prisoners of war, but as this information is furnished by countries with which we are at war, the War Department is helpless to expedite such reports.

The personal effects of an individual missing overseas are held by his unit for a period of time and are then sent to the Effects Quartermaster, Kansas City, Missouri, for disposition as designated by the soldier.

Permit me to extend to you my heartfelt sympathy during this period of uncertainty.

Sincerely yours,

J. A. ULIO
Major General
The Adjutant General

1 Inclosure
Bulletin of Information

Notification from War Department 2/2/45

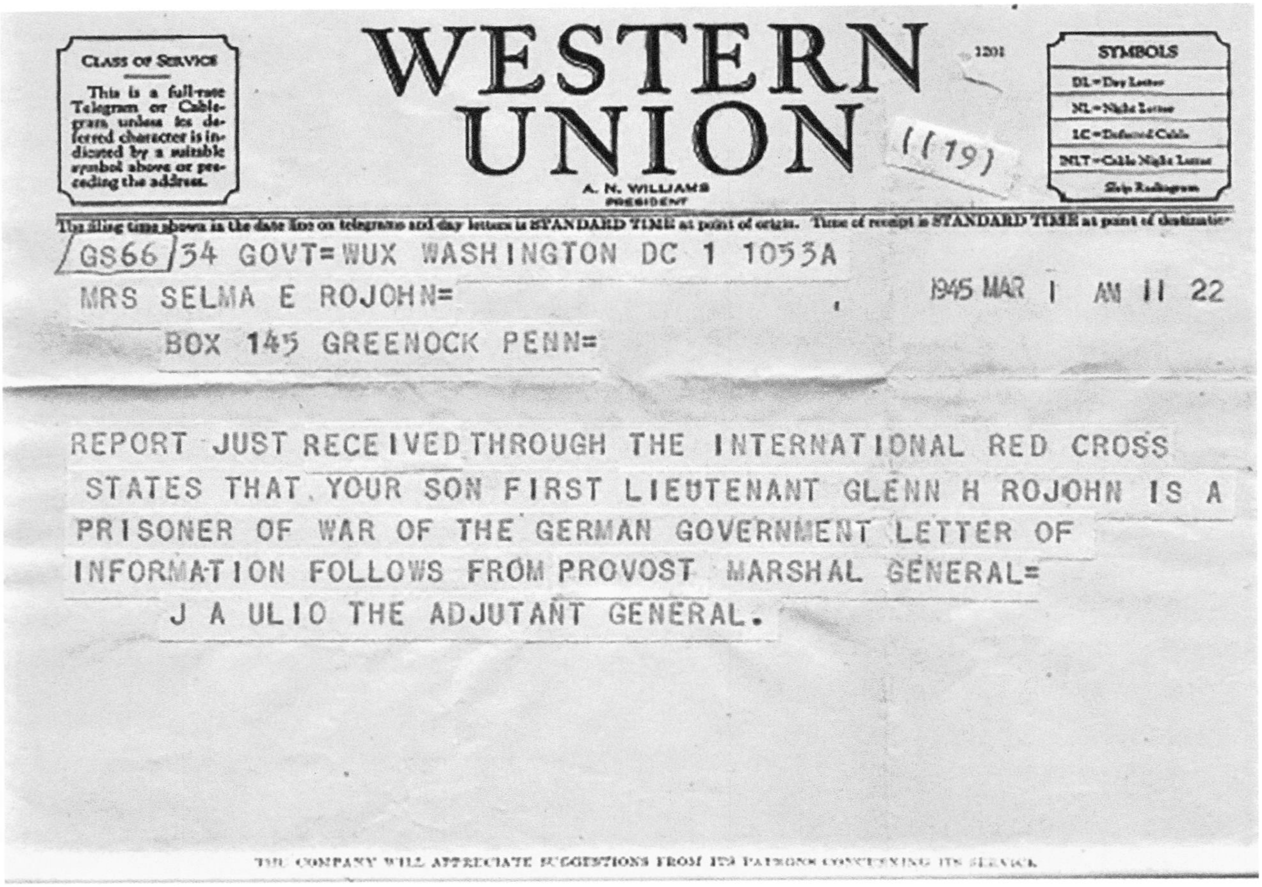

CLASS OF SERVICE

This is a full-rate Telegram or Cablegram unless its deferred character is indicated by a suitable symbol above or preceding the address.

WESTERN UNION

A. N. WILLIAMS
PRESIDENT

1201

(119)

SYMBOLS
DL = Day Letter
NL = Night Letter
LC = Deferred Cable
NLT = Cable Night Letter
Ship Radiogram

The filing time shown in the date line on telegrams and day letters is STANDARD TIME at point of origin. Time of receipt is STANDARD TIME at point of destination

GS66 34 GOVT=WUX WASHINGTON DC 1 1053A

MRS SELMA E ROJOHN= 1945 MAR 1 AM 11 22

BOX 145 GREENOCK PENN=

REPORT JUST RECEIVED THROUGH THE INTERNATIONAL RED CROSS STATES THAT YOUR SON FIRST LIEUTENANT GLENN H ROJOHN IS A PRISONER OF WAR OF THE GERMAN GOVERNMENT LETTER OF INFORMATION FOLLOWS FROM PROVOST MARSHAL GENERAL=

J A ULIO THE ADJUTANT GENERAL.

THE COMPANY WILL APPRECIATE SUGGESTIONS FROM ITS PATRONS CONCERNING ITS SERVICE

Telegram Notification POW 3/1/45

Lieut. Rojohn Safe

The War Department also notified relatives of First Lieut. Glenn E. Rojohn of Greenock, previously listed as missing, that he is a prisoner of war in Germany.

Pvt. Rybka   **Lieut. Rojohn**

Pvt. Rybka, a member of the 104th Infantry, had completed his seventh month of overseas service. A student at East McKeesport High School, he entered the army in June, 1943, and trained at Camp Robinson, Ark.

He was a former employee of the Carnegie-Illinois Steel Corp.'s Irvin Works.

He is survived by his mother, Mrs. Domicela Rybka, Fite Station; his wife, Veronica; three sisters, Josephine Dunlay, Ceotlia Kovak and Emelia Dziepack, and one brother, Theodore, private first class serving with the army in the Pacific.

Bomber Shot Down

Lieut. Rojohn, son of Mr. and Mrs. Harry D. Rojohn, Greenock, also had been listed as missing since Dec. 31 after his bomber was shot down during a mission over Germany. He is believed to have been on his 23rd bombing mission.

Lieut. Rojohn is a holder of the Air Medal and other awards for "exceptionally meritorious achievements" while piloting bombers for attacks on such vital targets as Berlin, Bremen, Leipzig and Ludwigshafen. He is a 1940 graduate of McKeesport High.

His brother, Leonard, also a first lieutenant, has completed 35 missions as a bomber pilot with the Eighth Air Force and now is on his way to the U. S., parents have been notified.

Newspaper announcement of POW status, also reporting Leonard Rojohn completed 35 missions is on way back to US

PRISONERS OF WAR LISTENING POST ASSN, ANTRIM N.H.
PLEASE ANSWER THIS CARD.   PHONE 15-12
-YOUR SON OR HUSBAND REPORTED A PRISONER OF WAR
VIA SHORT WAVE RADIO FROM GERMANY. 3/ 6 1725 P.M
SOLDIERS NAME _Glen H. Roehlen_ RANK 1.LT. WOUNDED _slight_
ARMY SERIAL# 0-F19292 NOT REPORTED _Call Jane_
ADDRESS IN GERMANY, "STALAG" LUFT # 1 .WRITE HIM,
SEE RED CROSS.***ADDRESSES AS GIVEN FROM BERLIN,
DUE TO ERRORS,ACCENT,& RADIO NOISE,REQUIRE MUCH
RESEARCH OF MAPS & ATLAS TO VERIFY TOWN NAMES TO
FIT MESSAGE.SOME FOLKS GET MANY CARDS IF ADDRESS
IS EASY,OTHERS ARE FORTUNATE TO GET ONE OTHERWISE.
WE MAIL HUNDREDS OF THESE CARDS TO ANXIOUS MOTHERS
& SWEETHEARTS,SO DONATIONS FOR POSTAGE BRING HAPP*
NESS & GLAD TIDINGS TO MANY OTHERS LIKE YOURSELF.

Shortwave Radio Transmission

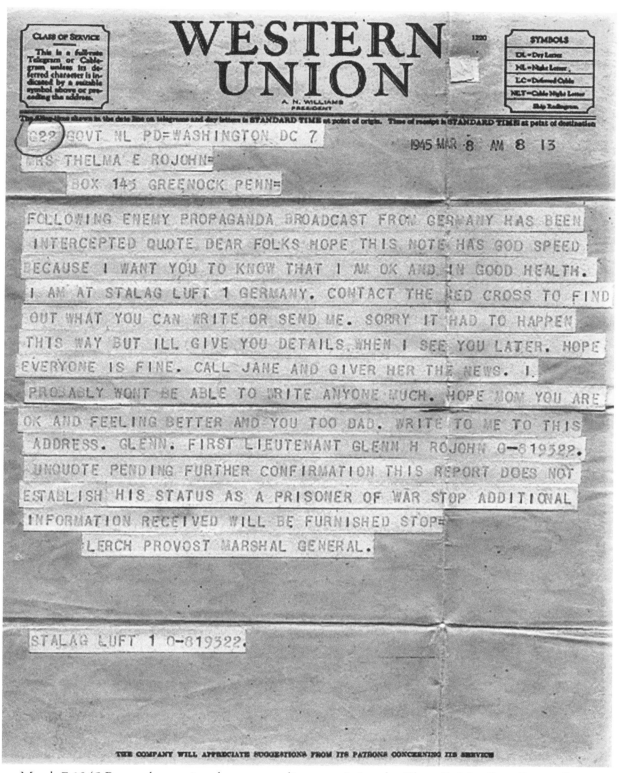

March 7 1945 Postcard reporting shortwave radio transmissions by Glenn Rojohn from Prison Camp

3/10/45

DEAR FOLKS: A NOTE TO YOU ALL THIS
MORNING. WHILE I'M WRITING THIS
YOU FOLKS ARE STILL SLEEPING.
WITH THE DIFFERENCE IN TIME YOU
REALIZE THAT WE A LONG WAY FROM
YOU ALL. SURE HOPE EVERYONE IS
FINE. I HAVE BEEN THINKING OF
YOU FOLKS ALOT LATELY HOPE
EVERYONE IS IN VERY GOOD HEALTH.
SOME ONE OF THESE DAYS I HOPE TO
WALK IN ON YOU AND SURPRISE YOU.
I HOPE MY CLOTHES AND PERSONAL
BELONGINGS HAVE REACHED HOME BY
NOW. HAVE BEEN THINKING OF YOU
NEW BUSINESS DAD. I HAVE HIGH PLANS
OF GETTING INTO SOMETHING WHEN I GET
BACK. POSSIBLY GO IN THE BANK AGAIN.

I CAN'T WRITE MANY LETTERS SO GIVE
EVERYONE MY REGARDS. WONDE IF
BETTY AND GLEN HAVE THE NEW BABY YET
GIVE MAURICE MY BEST. HOPE BROTHER
LEN GOT HOME FOR HIS BIRTHDAY.
I AM OK UNDER THE CIRCUMSTANCES. DON'T
WORRY. HOPE YOU HAVE HEARD FROM ME LOVE
GLENN

Letter from Prison Camp March 10, 1945

HEADQUARTERS ARMY SERVICE FORCES

OFFICE OF THE PROVOST MARSHAL GENERAL   tmw

WASHINGTON 25, D. C.

13 March 1945

RE: 1st Lt. Glenn H. Rojohn
United States Prisoner of War
Stalag Luft 1, Germany
Via: New York, New York

Mrs. Selma E. Rojohn
Box 145
Greenock, Pennsylvania

Dear Mrs. Rojohn:

The Provost Marshal General has directed me to inform you that the above-named prisoner of war has been reported interned at the place indicated.

You may communicate with him by following instructions in the inclosed circular.

One parcel label and two tobacco labels will be forwarded to you every sixty days without application on your
part. Labels for the current period will be forwarded under
separate cover with the least practicable delay.

Further information will be forwarded as soon as
it is received.

Sincerely yours,

Howard F. Bresee

2 Incls.   HOWARD F. BRESEE
Mail Instr   Colonel, CMP
Infor Circ   Director, American Prisoner of War
Information Bureau

MARCH 13, 1945 FAMILY INSTRUCTIONS HOW TO COMMUNICATE WITH A POW MEMBER

DEAR FOLKS: HERE I AM AGAIN. ITS HARD
TO FIND ANYTHING TO WRITE ABOUT
BUT I WANT TO LET YOU KNOW
EVERY CHANCE I GET THAT I'M STILL
OK. I WON'T BE ABLE TO WRITE JANE
THIS TIMES SO GIVE HER THE NEWS.
ALSO CLARENCE & MARGARET AND THE
REST. DO YOU REMEMBER HOW I USED
TO EAT BACK HOME. I THINK I'LL BE
TWICE AS BAD WHEN I GET BACK. MOM
YOU BETTER GET ALL YOU OLD & NEW
RECEIPIES OUT BECAUSE I'M GOING TO
RUN THE KITCHEN. DAD I HOPE THE
BUSINESS IS COMMING ALONG FINE. I'VE
HAD PLENTY OF TIME TO DO NOTHING BUT
THINK LATELY SO I'VE DEVELOPED SOME
FUTURE PLANS. IF I DON'T GO BACK TO

THE BANK. I WOULD LIKE TO GET IN SOME
SORT OF BUSINESS PREFERABLY WITH YOU. I'LL
HAVE SOME MONEY SAVED. I SURE HOPE YOU
ARE FEELING FINE MOM. I HAVE BEEN WORRIED
ABOUT YOU AND DAD. GOD WILLING I HOPE
TO SEE YOU ALL AGAIN BEFORE TOO LONG
A TIME. SO LONG FOR NOW   LOVE · GLENN.

Letter from Prison Camp 3/25/45

3/28/45

DEAR FOLKS: HERE I AM AGAIN. HOPE EVERYONE IS FINE AND DANDY. SURE HAVE BEEN WORRIED ABOUT YOU ALL. IF I JUST COULD HEAR THAT EVERYONE IS OK. I AM STILL PRETTY GOOD BUT DON'T WORRY ABOUT ME AT ALL. WE HAD OUR FIRST REAL SPRING DAY TODAY. I HAVE BEEN OUTSIDE MOST OF THE DAY GETTING A LITTLE OF SUNSHINE. IT SURE FELT GOOD TO BE ABLE TO SHEAD A FEW CLOTHES AFTER THE WINTER. I HAVE BEEN MAKING A SCRAP-BOOK WITH ODDS & END IN IT. I INCLUDED ALL THE THINGS I WANT YOU TO LOOK AT WHEN I GET BACK. YOU SHOULD SEE IT. YOU ARE IN FOR A JOB. SURE HOPE YOU ARE OK DAD. HAVE BEEN DOING A LOT OF THINKING ABOUT YOU AND MOM. GOT SOME IDEAS FOR YOU ALL WHEN I SEE YOU. CALL JANE FOR

ME AND GIVE HER MY LOVE. I HAVE BEEN WRITING ALL MY ALLOTTED LETTERS TO YOU. I HAVE BEEN WONDERING A LOT ABOUT LEONARD I CAN'T WRITE BUT I HOPE HE IS HOME WITH YOU ALL BY NOW. GIVE EVERYONE MY REGARDS AND I HOPE TO SEE YOU ALL. TAKE IT EASY AND PLEASE DON'T WORRY. MUCH LOVE - GLENN
Glenn

Letter 3/28/45 from Stalag Luft I

Memorabilia from Prison Camp taken when German's left camp

CHAPTER 7

HOME AT LAST

The European Theater was over. The Russians were in position to take over the German land and the citizens desecrated by the war. The United States Prisoners of War did not want to be released to the Russians fearing they would never be released. When word got out the war was ending, it was negotiated by Hubert "Hub" Zemke, senior American Officer that the Germans who were assigned to the camp that they leave in the middle of the night so they would not be captured by the Russians standing guard outside the camp.

A pact was made among those encamped in Stalag Luft I. "We only wanted to be released to our own." It took Zemke a few days to get their release organized. The airman still on base had one more mission… GET THE POWs OUT OF STALAG LUFT I. During the wait, the US servicemen had time to get records and souvenirs. Lt. Glenn H. Rojohn was able to find his POW record and a few reminders of his enemy. His POW record (Chapter 6 document) and Swastika bands (Chapter 6 document). They found Red Cross boxes stacked in the German quarters. The rations the POWs begged their loved ones to send to them because they were starving actually WERE sent. The Germans rationed them amongst themselves giving the POWs very little to survive on. Now they could have a feast while waiting to be rescued.

YouTube has posted the evacuation of Stalag Luft I. B-17s were lined up to take the POWs home. Lt. Glenn Rojohn wrote his family the letter he had been waiting to write since he was captured December 31, 1944—I have been liberated. [Document 1 at end of the chapter] The American Red Cross also notified his family of the liberation.

No documentation could be found of how Lt. Glenn H. Rojohn arrived back in the States, only that he had been processed in North Carolina and another notation of Fort Dix.

Glenn's parents were anxiously waiting for their son's arrival.

167

His mother made sure he was well fed. She made him all the dishes he asked for in his letters and tried a few new recipes he got from the men he made friends with while he was at War. He and his brother, the two Bomber Pilots, deserved some R & R. They often could be found napping in the living room.

The only connection Glenn had to war was the status documentation he received that can be found at the end of this chapter. Then a letter came in the mail from John Nilsson addressed to Lt. Glenn H. Rojohn, which can be seen at the back of this chapter. Nilsson was writing a book about the 100th Bomb Group in World War II. He wanted information on the Pick-a-Back incident that occurred December 31, 1944. Lt. Glenn H. Rojohn was forced to relive the memory of the day he and his crew almost died over the North Sea. THE STORY OF THE CENTURY today is a searched after collectable.

Lt. Glenn H. Rojohn decided to take off his wings and his medals. He decided to display them like a framed picture rather than continue a career in the military or as a pilot. The war was too much for him. He decided to pursue the ideas he thought about during those long hours at Stalag Luft I.

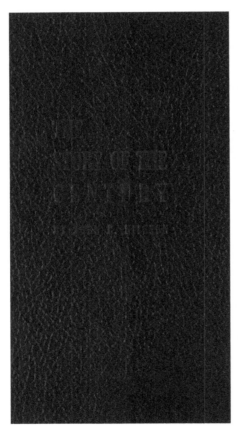

Story of the Century John R Nilsson   How Glenn H Rojohn displayed his medals

Documents in Chapter 7

Dear Folks:

Free men again. I hope by this time the War Dept has notified you that we have been liberated and are OK. I hope very much to beat this letter home but in case I don't you will know that I'm fine and dandy. We are eating pretty well again and all the boys are starting to look a little back to normal again. We are patiently waiting for transport out of here and back home. The boys have been roaming around hunting souvenirs. I doubt very much if all the letters I've written in the last month have ever gotten to you but I will write this one person before long. I had some good news the other day. I ran into a fellow who knew brother Jim. He told me that he went to school in France. That sure did perk me up. Give everyone my regards. Jim was homesick the other day when I had all the celebrating going on. Call Jane for me. I doubt if I will write her today. Until I see you so long.

Love
Glenn

Glenn Rojohn's Letter of being liberated

AMERICAN RED CROSS

PITTSBURGH CHAPTER
WABASH STATION
LIBERTY AVENUE AT PERRY STREET
PITTSBURGH 22, PENNSYLVANIA
Telephone—GRant 1680

HOME SERVICE DEPARTMENT
239 FOURTH AVENUE
Telephone GRant 4930

May 25, 1945

Mrs. Selma E. Rojohn
Box 145
Greenock, Pa.

Dear Mrs. Rojohn:

We thought you would like to have a copy of the message from Lt. Rojohn which has been given to you by telephone. The wire said:

"May 22, 1945, Lt. Glenn N. Rojohn, 0819322, requests Selma E. Rojohn, Box 145, Greenock, be notified his liberation."

This cable was sent through the American Red Cross as part of a new Red Cross service being offered to liberated prisoners of war in order to supplement official notification of liberation and to hasten reports to families.

Sincerely yours,

Mrs. Richard C. Carr
Prisoner of War Service

American Red Cross letter of liberation

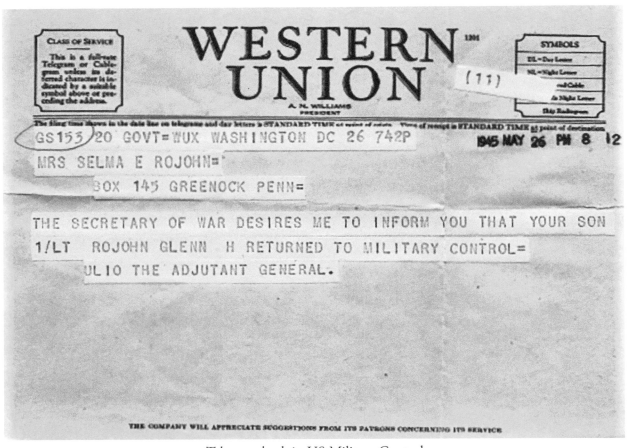

Telegram back in US Military Control

WESTERN UNION

1201

A. N. WILLIAMS
PRESIDENT

.(25)

The filing time shown in the date line on telegrams and day letters is STANDARD TIME at point of origin. Time of receipt is STANDARD TIME at point of destination

GS62 41 GOVT=WASHINGTON DC 20 259A

MRS SELMA E ROJOHN=

BOX 145 GREENOCK PENN=

1945 JUN 20 AM 9 2

THE CHIEF OF STAFF OF THE ARMY DIRECTS ME TO INFORM YOU
YOUR SON 1/LT ROJOHN GLENN H IS BEING RETURNED TO THE
UNITED STATES WITHIN THE NEAR FUTURE AND WILL BE GIVEN
AN OPPORTUNITY TO COMMUNICATE WITH YOU UPON ARRIVAL =

J A ULIO THE ADJUTANT GENERAL.

1/LT GREENOCK.

THE COMPANY WILL APPRECIATE SUGGESTIONS FROM ITS PATRONS CONCERNING ITS SERVICE

Being Returned to the US

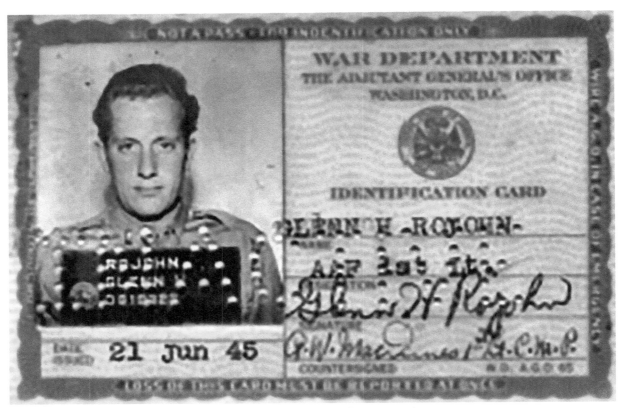

War Department Identification card

1. LAST NAME	FIRST NAME	MIDDLE NAME	2. SERIAL NUMBER
ROJOHN	Glenn	Harry	O819322

3. BIRTH DATE	4. PLACE OF BIRTH	5. CITIZEN (Date Natur. or No.)	6. RACE
6Apr1922	Pennsylvania		W

7. MARITAL STATUS	9. DEPENDENTS		10. PARENTS EXTRACTION OR NATIONALITY		
Single	Relationship	No.		Nationality	U.S. Citizen
			Father	American	Born

8. RELIGION				
Lutheran		Mother	American	Born

11. HEIGHT	12. WEIGHT	13. COLOR HAIR	14. COLOR EYES	15. GLASSES (Reason)
6' 1"	195	Blonde	Blue	

16. EMERGENCY ADDRESSEE

FULL NAME: Mrs Selman E (Berthiaume) Rojohn   RELATIONSHIP: Mother

STREET ADDRESS: Box 145   CITY: Greenock Pa   STATE:

17. EDUCATION					
Level	Name of School	Years Att'd	Date Grad.	Major Subject	Degree
HS	Robert Morris Sch of Accounting, Pittsburgh, Pa.	1½	1942	Accounting	NG

18. SIGNATURE OF OFFICER

19. OFFICIAL SIGNATURE OF CLASSIFICATION OFFICER

JOHN M CARNEY, Maj, AC   AAFFS #5 G'boro,NC   DATE 9Oct45

20. DUTY ARM OR SERVICE
AC

21. DATE E.A.D.	AUTHORITY	
7Jan44	Par 14, SO 6, Hq. AAF Pilot Sch Stuttgart, Ark. 6Jan44	

22. PERM. ADDRESS OR PLACE FROM WHICH ORDERED TO E.A.D. (City & State)	23. DATE OF ACTIVE SERVICE
Greenock, Pa.	7Jan44

24. LIMITED SERVICE (Details)	AUTHORITY	DATE
	QUALIFIED FOR DUTY	

25. RETIRED (Reason)	GRADE	DATE

26. RETURN FROM OVERSEAS (Give Exact Reason)	DATE
Liberated POW	20Jun45

27. COMMISSION AND APPOINTMENT DATA

Component	Arm or Serv.	Grade Appt'd	Date Comm.	Comm. From	Disenrolled — Grade, Date & Reason
(A) PRESENT APPOINTMENT					
AUS	AC	2d Lt	7Jan 1944	AFFS	

(B) PREVIOUS APPOINTMENTS NOT CONTINUED, OTHER BRANCHES ARMED SERV. & FOREIGN MIL. ESTAB.

28. PROMOTION RECORD (From Date Present Appointment — See 27 (A))

E. A. Form 66—W. C.	GRADE				DATE		ORDERS
	AC — '34	A. U. S.	AC — '42	Other	Effective	Rank	
	2d Lt				7Jan 1944	7Jan 1944	Ref 21
	1st Lt				Oct 1944	Oct 1944	No Auth.

WD AGO Form 66-2 2 July 1948

30. SPECIAL AND GENERAL SERVICE SCHOOLS AND SCHOOLS FOR SPECIALIZED TRAINING				
NAME AND PLACE OF SCHOOL OR STATION	Length of Course	Yes or No	Date	DESCRIPTION OF COURSE
PFS, Maxwell Fld, Ala	2mo	Yes	Jun43	Pre flt pilot tng
FTD, McBride Fld, Chester, Miss.	2mo	Yes	Aug43	Primary pilot tng
BFS, Malden, Miss.	2mo	Yes	Oct43	Basic Pilot tng
AFS, Stuttgart, Ark.	2mo	Yes	Jan44	Adv TE Pilot tng
Chanute Fld, Ill	2mo	Yes	Mar44	Trans B-17 tng.

33. RECOMMEND FOR DUTY OR QUALIFIED IN M. O. S.

1091 Pilot B-17
1024 Pilot 4 Eng.

34. REMARKS
No 66-1 or 66-2 available at Greensboro, N.C. 9Oct45

'CERTIFIED TRUE COPY'

MAURICE GOLDBERG, Capt, AC, 9Oct45

PERSONNEL ORDERS: RATINGS, FLYING STATUS   P31 (pilot) P31 (Fly Status) PO59, Hq. AAFEFTC, Maxwell Fld, Ala. 31Dec43, eff 7Jan44

68-No

AAF OFFICERS' QUALIFICATION RECORD

WDAGO form 66-2

176

1. LAST NAME	FIRST NAME	MIDDLE NAME	2. SERIAL NUMBER	R				29. DUTY ARM OR SERVICE
ROJOHN	Glenn	Harry	0819322					AC
3. BIRTH DATE	4. PLACE OF BIRTH	5. CITIZEN (Dole Nolhr. or No)	6. RACE					

33. AIR CREW DATA   22 cbt mis, 180 cbt hrs, 9Oct45

(A) FLYING STATUS		(B) DATE OF ACTIVE SERVICE			(E) TYPE EXPERIENCE AND TYPE EQUIPMENT						
X			7Jan44			PERSUIT	BOMBER	DIVE	OTHER	TRANSPORT	APPROXIMATE INCL DATES	AREA
F	NF			TACTICAL-COMBAT			B-17				Aug44-Dec44	ETO
(C) FLYING RESTRICTIONS				TACTICAL — NONCOMBAT			B-17				Mar44 Apr44	USA
Date	Length	Reasons		TRAINING			B-17		PT17,BT13,15 AT10		Jun43 Mar44	USA
(D) PILOT ENGINE QUALIFICATIONS				OTHER								
Engines		Date of Qualifications		(F) FLYING HOURS				36. CIVILIAN FLYING EXPERIENCE			
Two 4-Engine				HOURS	APPROXIMATE DATES		HOURS	TYPE EQUIPMENT	E. P.	HOURS	NATURE OF ACTIVITY
4-Engine				— 250			1,000 — 1,500				
2-Engine				250 — 500			1,500 — 2,000				
1-Engine				500 — 750	Dec44		2,000 — 3,000				
				750 — 1,000			+ 3,000				

(A) AIR CORPS RATINGS													37. AIR FORCE SPECIALTIES		(B) RATED, NONPILOT SPECIALTIES						
P	SP	CP	GP	LP	SSP	ISSP	BP	TBP	AO	SAO	TO			NAV.	BOM.	GUN.	ARMR.	WEA.	ENGR.	COM.	PHOTO.
X																					

APPROXIMATE INCL. DATES	TYPE AND NUMBER OF ORGANIZATION AND LOCATION	POSITION AND DESCRIPTION OF DUTIES (Incl. Type Equipment and Approx. Flying Hours Where Applicable)	PERFORMANCE RATING	OCCUPATIONAL CODE AND TITLE (AR 600-95)
24Oct42-4Apr43	EM Pvt- Recruiting Duty, Pitts., Pa.			
5Apr43-6Jan44	A/C tng (Ref 30) PT-17 (75hrs), BT-13 (85hrs), AT-10 (100hrs)			
7Jan44 23Mar44	AAF Chanute Fld, Ill	Pilot B-17 Trans Tng. 110 hrs		1024 Pilot 4 Eng
24Mar44 24Apr44	AAF Delhart, Tex	Pilot B-17 RTU 40 hrs		1092 Pilot B-17
25Apr44 28Jun44	AAB Gulf Port, Miss.	Pilot B-17 RTU 95 hrs		1092 Pilot B-17
29Jun44 11Aug44	AAF Langley Va.	Pilot B-17 Mission Pilot 50 hrs		1092 Pilot B-17
12Aug44 19Aug44	USA and Enroute	Pilot B-17 Departed US 15Aug44 23 hrs		1092 Pilot B-17
20Aug44 31Dec44	350 Bomb Sq, 100 B. Gp 8AF ETOUSA, England	Pilot B-17, 22 cbt mis, 130 cbt hrs, 250 tot hrs.		
31Dec44 13May45	Germany	Project "R" (POW)		To be assigned in accordance with AAF ltr 35-228A
14May45	AAFRS #5	Return to US, Leave and processing ordered to	UNK JMC	

WDAGO form 66-2

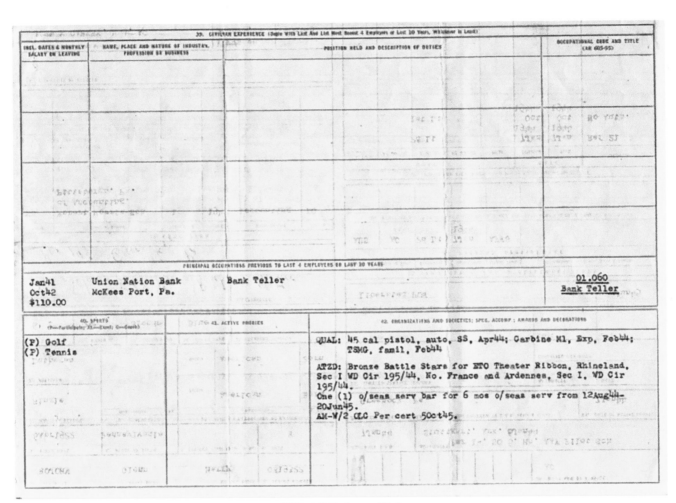

WDAGO form 66-2

D-30/GR 2-A   TEMPORARY WDAGO FORM 66-1

PW CAMP LUFT #1   Name RONJOHN GLENN H Rank 1st Lt   ASN O-819???
(Stalag No.Lib.Ea.Ev   (Last)   (First)   (Init)

                                                    Address of   BOX # 145
                                                    resuperation   Street & No.
Unit (/NNDB#) 350 BS AC Date 30 MAY 45   MCS   GREENOCK, PENNA
(Former unit & arm of Serv.)(Date of return US Cont'l)   (City & State
                              13/5/45
Reception
Station FORT DIX #2.   Date of Capture 31/12/44 PW Number 7403 Religion P Race W
(Station)(Code No.)

Date of Rank 25/10/44 Type of Duty PILOT Foreign Service From
                                          1/6/45   0/00.88 (Date Ent'd) (Where)
                                          Due U.S. F/P 500-70 U.E. Reichmuth Jr Capt
Immunized: TYPHUS 31/5/45 BLOOD O Sym. No. 211-268 94 Fin Disb Sec LWC FD
         (Type) (Date) (Type) (Date)

Legal Residence
              (Street)   (City or Town)   (State)

Emergency
Addressee SELMA F RONJOHN (MOTHER) BOX # 145 GREENOCK   PENND
        (Name) (Relationship) (Street)   (City or Town)   (State)
           P.P. (NO)

AAF   RANDOLPH M. GALLON
                                           1st Lt.   TC
                                           Acts Asst Ad j Gen.

Temporary WDGO Form 66-1

CERTIFICATE OF SERVICE

1. LAST NAME - FIRST NAME - MIDDLE INITIAL	2. ARMY SERIAL NUMBER	3. ADV. GRADE	4. ARM OR SERVICE	5. COMPONENT
RO JOHN GLENN H	0819322	1st Lt	AC	AUS

6. ORGANIZATION	7. DATE OF RELIEF FROM ACTIVE DUTY	8. PLACE OF SEPARATION
350 Bomb Sq 100 Bomb Gp APO 559 New York	27 Nov 45	AAF ORD GREENSBORO N C

9. PERMANENT ADDRESS FOR MAILING PURPOSES	10. DATE OF BIRTH	11. PLACE OF BIRTH
Box 145 Greenock Pa	6 Apr 1922	Pa

12. ADDRESS FROM WHICH EMPLOYMENT WILL BE SOUGHT	13. COLOR EYES	14. COLOR HAIR	15. HEIGHT	16. WEIGHT	17. NO. OF DEPENDENTS
See 9	Blue	Blond	6'1"	195	0

18. RACE			19. MARITAL STATUS			20. U.S.CITIZEN		21. CIVILIAN OCCUPATION AND NO.
WHITE	NEGRO	OTHER	SINGLE	MARRIED	OTHER	YES	NO	Bank Teller
X				X		X		

MILITARY HISTORY

	22. REGISTERED	23. LOCAL B. B. BOARD NUMBER	24. COUNTY AND STATE	25. HOME ADDRESS AT TIME OF ENTRY ON ACTIVE DUTY
SELECTIVE SERVICE DATA	YES X NO		Allegheny Pa	See 9

26. DATE OF ENTRY ON ACTIVE DUTY	27. MILITARY OCCUPATIONAL SPECIALTY AND NO.
7 Jan 44	1091 Pilot B-17

28. BATTLES AND CAMPAIGNS
Rhineland Northern France Ardennes

29. DECORATIONS AND CITATIONS
ETO Theater Ribbon with 3 Battle Stars
Air Medal with 2 Oak Leaf Clusters 1 Overseas Service Bar

30. WOUNDS RECEIVED IN ACTION
NONE

31. SERVICE SCHOOLS ATTENDED	32. SERVICE OUTSIDE CONTINENTAL U. S. AND RETURN		
PFS Maxwell Fld Ala Chanute Fld Ill Trans RTU Delhart Tex	DATE OF DEPARTURE	DESTINATION	DATE OF ARRIVAL
FTD McBride Fld Chester Miss Gulfport Miss	15 Aug 44	England	20 Jun 45
BFS Malden Miss AFS Stuttgart Ark Langley Fld Va-Radar Nav Tng			

33. REASON AND AUTHORITY FOR SEPARATION
See 43

34. CURRENT TOUR OF ACTIVE DUTY						35. EDUCATION (years)		
CONTINENTAL SERVICE			FOREIGN SERVICE			GRAMMAR SCHOOL	HIGH SCHOOL	COLLEGE
YEARS	MONTHS	DAYS	YEARS	MONTHS	DAYS	8	4	1½
1	0	15	0	10	5			

INSURANCE NOTICE

36. KIND OF INSURANCE			37. HOW PAID			38. Effective Date of Allotment Discontinuance	39. Date of Next Premium (one month after 38)	40. PREMIUM DUE EACH MONTH	41. INTENTION OF VETERAN TO		
Nat. Serv.	U.S. Govt.	None	Allotment	Direct to V.A.					Continue	Continue only	Discontinue
X				X		31 Oct 45	30 Nov 45	6.50	X		

43. REMARKS
WD Readjustment Reg 1-5 AAF Ltr 155-9 TWX AFPMP-2559 Hq AAF dated 15 Aug 45 & Ltr Hq AAF Subj: "AAF Separation Bases" dated 6 Sep 45

Lapel Button issued

45. PERSONNEL OFFICER
G E BAGWELL Capt A C

Certificate of Service WDAGO Form 53 98

CITATION FOR THE DISTINGUISHED FLYING CROSS

First Lieutenant Glenn H. Rojohn, 0819322, Air Corps, Army of the United States. For extraordinary achievement while participating in aerial flight on 31 December 1944. While over the North Sea, returning from a combat mission over Hamburg, Germany, Lieutenant Rojohn's aircraft became locked atop another in a mid-air collision caused by violent evasive action. Displaying keen presence of mind and coolness in the face of grave danger, Lieutenant Rojohn quickly cut the switches to his engines and, using the controls of his plane and the engines of the other, headed the aircraft towards land. Upon reaching land, Lieutenant Rojohn ordered his crew to abandon his plane and then maneuvered the aircraft to a successful crash landing. Lieutenant Rojohn's extraordinary flying ability and his courageous action reflect great credit upon himself and the Army Air Forces.

Copy of Citation for The Distinguished Flying Cross Original not found

HEADQUARTERS
AAF OVERSEAS REPLACEMEMT DEPOT
AND AAF REDISTRIBUTION STATION No. 5
GREENSBORO, NORTH CAROLINA
OFFICE OF THE COMMANDING OFFICER

In Reply
Refer to 201 - Rojohn, Glenn H.   10 Oct 45

SUBJECT: Appointment under Section 37,
           National Defense Act, as amended

TO: 1st Lt. Glenn H. Rojohn, AC Res   A 1st Lt., Air Corps
    Box #145
    Greenock, Pennsylvania   B O 819 322

    1. The Secretary of War has directed me to inform you
that by direction of the President, you are tendered appointment in the Officers' Reserve Corps, Army of the United
States, effective this date, in the grade and section shown
after A above. Your serial number is shown after B above.

    2. There is inclosed herewith a form for oath of office,
which you are requested to execute and return promptly to
the agency from which it was received by you. The execution
and return of the required oath of office constitute an acceptance of your appointment. No other evidence of acceptance
is required. Upon receipt in the War Department of the oath
of office, properly executed, a commission evidencing your
appointment will be sent to you.

    3. Prompt action is requested since the regulations
require cancellation of the tender of appointment if acceptance is not received within a reasonable time.

    4. You will not perform the duties of an officer under
this appointment until specifically so directed by compe-
tent orders.

    5. Whenever your permanent address is changed, it is
important that you notify all concerned, using the inclosed
Personal Report form.

PAUL R. YOUNTS
Colonel, Air Corps
Commanding

2 Incls
  1. Form for Oath of Office
  2. Personal Report Form

Appointment to the Officers Reserved corps

Honorable Discharge

from the Armed Forces of the United States of America

This is to certify that

FIRST LIEUTENANT GLENN H. ROJOHN, AO 819 322, AIR FORCE RESERVE

was Honorably Discharged from the

United States Air Force

on the FIFTEENTH day of MARCH 1957 This certificate is awarded as a testimonial of Honest and Faithful Service

JOE L. FERNANDES
MAJOR, USAF

DD FORM 256 AF PREVIOUS EDITIONS OF THIS FORM MAY BE USED.
1 NOV 51

Honorable Discharge

AIR RESERVE RECORDS CENTER
CONTINENTAL AIR COMMAND
5800 YORK STREET
DENVER 5, COLORADO

CG-CR2a   Rojohn, Glenn H., AO 819 322   9 JUN 1955

SUBJECT: Report of Total Allowable Points and Service

TO: 1st Lt Glenn H. Rojohn
             829 Pinecrest Avenue
             Mc Keesport, Pennsylvania

   1.   Under the provisions of AFR 35-71 this Center is required to
furnish you a computation of allowable points and service creditable
for Reserve retirement. This information is contained in Section II of
your AF Form 712.

   2.   The inclosed AF Form 712 is your record of creditable service
as of the last date indicated. All points and service shown are inclusive of creditable information contained in your military records or
provided by you.

   3.   If you have further inquiries relative to points or creditable
service, address your communication to this Center, attention: CG-CR2a.

          BY ORDER OF THE COMMANDER:

1 Incl   PRICE D. RICE
AF Form 712   Major, USAF
                                              Chief, Credits Division

Allowable Points and Service Report

AIR FORCE RESERVE PERSONNEL REPORT OF TOTAL ALLOWABLE POINTS AND SERVICE								

I. PERSONNEL DATA

1. LAST NAME - FIRST NAME - MIDDLE INITIAL	2. SERVICE NO.	3. RESERVE GRADE	4. DATE OF BIRTH
Rojohn, Glenn H. AO	819 322	1st Lt	6 Apr 22

5. DATE (indicate day, month and year, "year of service for retirement" begins)	6. DATES (indicate day, month and year "year of service for rotation" begins)				
26 May 55	A. 26 May 55	B.	C.	D.	E.
	F.	G.	H.	I.	J.

II. ALLOWABLE POINTS AND FEDERAL SERVICE

	ACTIVE DUTY POINTS A	INACTIVE DUTY POINTS B	GRATUITOUS POINTS C	TOTAL POINTS D	RETIREMENT POINTS E	SATISFACTORY FEDERAL SERVICE		
						YEARS F	MONTHS G	DAYS H
7. ALLOWABLE FEDERAL SERVICE PRIOR TO 1 JULY 1949.	1131	183		1314	1314	6	9	4
8. RESERVE SERVICE (Subsequent to 30 June 1949 to date "year of service for retirement" begins)	0	0	86	86	86	0	0	0
9. REGULAR SERVICE (Subsequent to 30 June 1949 to date "year of service" begins)								
10. ANNUAL ENTRIES FROM AF FORM 110 (By "year of service for retirement")								
DATES								
FROM	TO							

Completed: 27 May 55 vcb

AF FORM 712

Allowable Points and Service Report

CAUTION: NOT TO BE USED FOR
IDENTIFICATION PURPOSES

ANY ALTERATIONS IN SHADED AREAS
RENDER FORM VOID

1. NAME (Last, first, middle)	2. DEPARTMENT, COMPONENT AND BRANCH	3. SOCIAL SECURITY NO. (Also, Service Number if applicable)
RO JOHN GLENN H	ARMY/AUS/AC	0 819 322

4. MAILING ADDRESS (Include ZIP Code)
BOX 145 GREENOCK PA

5. ORIGINAL DD FORM 214 IS CORRECTED AS INDICATED BELOW

ITEM NO.	WD AGO 53-98	CORRECTED TO READ

SEPARATION DATE ON RECORD BEING CORRECTED - XXXXXXXX ___ 27 NOV 45 ___

3   CAPT
29   ADD: DISTINGUISHED FLYING CROSS//PURPLE HEART//POW MEDAL//AMERICAN CAMPAIGN
     MEDAL//WORLD WAR II VICTORY MEDAL
30   DELETE: NONE
     ADD: 31 DEC 44 EUROPEAN THEATER
43   ADD: POW 350TH BOMB SQUADRON 100TH BOMB GROUP GERMANY 31 DEC 44-1 MAY 45//
     NOTHING FOLLOWS

6. DATE	7. TYPED NAME, GRADE, TITLE AND SIGNATURE OF OFFICIAL AUTHORIZED TO SIGN
21 Aug 1998	LISA M SANDOR GS7 MIL PERS STAT TECH ARBA-SL

DD FORM 215 1 JUL 79

PREVIOUS EDITIONS OF THIS FORM ARE OBSOLETE.

CORRECTION TO DD FORM 214, CERTIFICATE OF RELEASE OR DISCHARGE FROM ACTIVE DUTY

S/N 0102-LF-000-2150

MEMBER - 1

DD 215 Correction to add Captain Status

100th Bombardment Group
Thorpe Abbotts, England

Dear Mr. Rojohn:

In a history of the 100th Group, which is now being prepared, we want to include some mention of the incident over -- or near -- Hamburg last December 31 when your Fort and another settled against one another and went down.

According to some of the fliers, both of the Forts were filling in the same gap in the formation, unaware the other was trying to do the same thing.

I understand the other Fort was that of Lt. William Macnab.

If it is not asking too much, I wonder if you could give me some of the details of this incident? For instance, what was said over VHF or the interphone at that moment? Isn't it true that several of the gunners bailed out into the sea?

It seems to me it was a pretty brilliant piece of work, heading both Forts back towards land, and I wonder how you managed to do that. Four of Macnab's crew, including Berkowitz, Comer, Woodall, and Chadwick, are now listed as Returned, and six of your crew, including yourself, Leek, Washington, Shirley, Neuhaus, and Elkin.

Did any of you stay in the Forts until they struck on the beach?

The History will contain stories of the Hamburg mission, as well as Regensburg, Bremen, Munster, Berlin, D-Day, St. Sylvain, Merseburg, Schweinfurt, and many others, with lists of crews lost and participating in many of the important missions as well as gunners with credit for destroyed planes, etc.

Sincerely

Cpl John R Nilsson

P.S.--If you didn't get a Luckye Bastardes certificate, mention it and I will send you one.

John R Nilsson Letter & envelope

187

NILSSON--PUBLIC RELATIONS OFFICE
100TH BOMBARDMENT GROUP
APO 557
% PM NY NY USA

Free

LT. GLENN R ROJOHN

BOX 146

GREENOCK, PA.   USA

SEP 24 1945

CHAPTER 8

LIFE AFTER THE WAR

Like other World War II Veterans, Glenn H. Rojohn looked at flying a B-17 as his job. "Just doing my job for my country." He took a little time off between his war time and getting on with his life. Glenn was not one that could sit around but he had to make some decisions what he wanted to do--go back to the bank or develop a family business that he thought about in those long hours at Stalag Luft I.

Glenn's father, Harry, started a heating & plumbing business with his cousin near their home in the mill town of McKeesport, PA when his sons were at war. Glenn decided to help develop a business with his family and add another Rojohn to Lacey & Rojohn Heating and Plumbing. Glenn is sitting at his new desk smoking one of his cigars. His salesmanship provided him trips around the world throughout his career.

Glenn H Rojohn starting his new career

He decided to continue his family's philosophy of service. He was a very active member of the local Kiwanis and Chamber of Commerce until he retired.

His role in the company grew into making connections to help grow the bottom line. That role gave him the opportunity of following two loves of his life—golf and tennis. His love of golf began at an early age as shown swinging clubs on the farm. They joined Youghiogheny Country Club in Elizabeth Township, PA to make business connections on the golf course. Not only could he play, he was really good at it. He achieved the goal everyone has, a hole in one at one of the hardest courses in the area. At one time he also had a very low handicap. So their sons could play tennis, his parents had built a clay court on the property where they lived before the war. Much later, Glenn was instrumental in building the tennis courts at Youghiogheny Country Club. His passion was to teach children the game he loved. He maintained his membership at YCC until neck and back issues prohibited him to play the games he played for almost all of his life.

Glenn and Leonard playing golf on the farm

McCormick family holiday gathering

The Glenn H Rojohn family

The family business expanded to include a merger with another family and a passion of Glenn and his brother Leonard. Peckman-Rojohn Lincoln Mercury was born. That business gave them a perk of bringing home a different Lincoln every night. During his time in the business he decided Jane and the family needed a new car. Ironically the Mercury station wagon he decided to purchase caught fire in the process of delivery to his home. Thank God it burst into flames on the dealer parking lot instead of the Rojohn driveway. That incident was and still is constant topic of discussion at family gatherings.

In 1946, he married the girl he met on a blind date, Jane McCormick, before he went to war. The country boy and the Pittsburgh city girl merged their families. Pictured in the home of Jane's mother are her brother in law John Wayman, nephew Jack, sister Marion, her mother Gertrude, Aunt Grace, Jane, and Glenn. Glenn and Jane raised a family in the town where he grew up. Shown in a picture taken in the late 60s are Glenn, Jane, daughter Cyndi, and son Dave. He coached Little League for his son's teams. If you would talk to his children's friends, they would tell you what they remembered most about him was he was the only YCC swim team parent with a station wagon. There were arguments amongst the team members as to who got to join the station wagon party to go to away swim meets. He and his wife enjoyed a robust social life with life long friends.

Sports were the love of his life. He purchased 4 Steelers season tickets for the 1946 season when he came home from war. He was one of the original members of STEELER NATION. He and his family enjoyed decades of gong to the home games together. They also gathered together for Super Bowl parties celebrating long awaited victories. His connection was strong enough that when owner Dan Rooney had a landing incident at Allegheny County Airport, Glenn wrote him a letter of concern for his well being based on the news reports. Dan Rooney responded with a note. Glenn never missed a game until Heinz field was built. There were just too many steps for the body of the ailing Veteran to climb. It was difficult for him and his family to watch the acknowledgement that his days of watching the game live were over. Glenn's family is still the proud owner of those four season tickets. The family will always have one regret, that when Glenn's days were numbered that they didn't call the Steelers office to have a team member come to make a visit to the World War II legend who was a decades long season ticket holder.

Baseball was a family pastime of that generation. That was also true of the Glenn Rojohn family. His parents spent hours listening to baseball games when he was growing up. Glenn coached all of his son's Little League teams. One of his son's fondest memories of his father and baseball was the trip they made to Forbes Field for the 1960 World Series. Sports were Glenn's passion.

In 1981 Glenn found a new competitive sport to love. He grew up along the Youghiogheny River. He always loved the water. His family made yearly trips to the beach from the time he was young. He was soon to retire so he decided to purchase 6 weeks at Time Share Native Sun Resort in Lauderdale by the Sea, Florida for his family to enjoy sun and surf. Somehow Glenn made shelling a competitive sport. He went out daily with his net to out do himself every day. Most days he got other owners involved in the "Lets see who can find the best shell" game. Glenn always won.

The true joys of his life were his Grandchildren. He found a new journey. His oldest, Nathan is a "special child". He did anything and everything in his power to make sure he was taken care of. Gavin inherited his love of sports. Like all kids his age, he loved video games. But he also loved golf and baseball. Glenn

Nathan Rojohn

Gavin Rojohn

Lexii Rojohn

taught him the fundamentals. He took him out to the driving range and batting cage. Glenn never missed one of Gavin's games. Gavin was always enamored with his Gross Pup's World War II story and helped with the research for this book. Lexii came later in Glenn's life. He bought her first bike and helped teach her to ride. She is the creative one. He made sure she was never without paint, crayons, markers and paper. She helped with the aesthetics elements of the book on his life in honor of her Grandfather.

Glenn H. Rojohn was a man of faith. His great grandfather founded the Lutheran Church in the town where he lived all his life. He served on Council at the church for decades. Captain Glenn H. Rojohn's life went on. The war was behind him. Or was it? His faith helped him through his life journeys so far. His faith will help him through life journeys to come.

CHAPTER 9

THE CREW'S RECONNECTION

All we knew growing up was that our father could not watch war movies, he needed every light on in the house, and never wanted rutabagas any where near the house. We also were aware from the time we were young that he was overly stressed. Now that we really know the story of Mission 22, we had and still have so many questions. Like so many Veterans, he didn't talk about the war. He never mentioned he was written in books. He never mentioned the Piggyback Flight. Once we learned about his experiences at his big reveal at the Allegheny County Warbirds Show lots of little things he did made more sense.

After Jane Rojohn died in 2009, the family found several cassette tapes among the Piggyback Flight memorabilia. They got tossed aside assuming they wouldn't play after 20+ years. In 2015 it was decided to try to play them

What a gift those tossed aside cassette tapes proved to be. They worked! And those cassettes were like they were recorded that day. Most importantly they provided so much information we didn't know.

For my brother and I, the one cassette that told us the most was the cassette that told us he received a letter from a former crew member of LT. Bill Macnab and a witness of the collision at a distance. He received that letter not long after the war ended. The letter accused the Piggyback Flight Pilot of being responsible for killing Lts Bill Macnab and Vaughn and crew members of both Nine Lives and The Little Skipper. He said that "Glenn Rojohn was responsible for the deaths and imprisonment of the crews of the two planes." An accusation that was later proved to have no merit.

For over forty years he carried that guilt and pain. My brother and I did not have the easiest time growing up. We just never seemed to have that bond with our parents that our friends had with their parents. We learned after Glenn's death that he spent much time with a therapist to help him with the guilt and

Little May Still Be Alive, Pilot Tells Parents

Lt. Glenn Rojohn, pilot of the Flying Fortress on which Staff Sgt. Roy Little served when he was reported missing in action, came from his home in Greenook, Pa., last week to visit Roy's parents, Mr. and Mrs. C. C. Little, 3700 E. Cudahy ave.

He said he had been mighty proud of his crew and was visiting the homes of three of the men who had been unaccounted for when they were all forced to ball out over the North Sea near Wilmshaven, Germany, on Dec. 31, 1944. Six of the men, including the pilot, were taken to German prison camps where they were held captive until their liberation by the Russians last May. Lt. Rojohn told how he searched prison hospitals and camps after his release in an effort to locate Roy and the other two missing men, as he believed they had a good chance of being alive, but his search proved unsuccessful.

Roy, age 21, was an engineer and waist gunner on the plane.

Rojohn meets Little family

193

pain. Unfortunately for us we did not find that letter in the memorabilia. Our thought was the therapist recommended he destroy it. We will always ask how our lives would be different had he not received that accusatory letter.

That letter was the beginning of another journey for Glenn H. Rojohn. He wanted to find his crew members and their families to apologize for what he was accused of being responsible for on December 31, 1944. We assume one of the psychologists who treated him, agreed that may help him. His first trip was to find the family of his waist gunner Roy Little as described in an article sent to us by Rich Hehn, Roy's cousin.

He sought help from the Social Security Administration for information and hired private investigators trying to find his crew. He wasn't having any luck finding his co-pilot, his friend Bill Leek. He didn't remember he sent his mother a letter with the addresses for his crew. (included at end of Chapter 3). Had he remembered the letter or addresses in his POW Diary, this journey could have been much easier. Today some asked why this was such a difficult process. Back in those days the sophisticated resources that there are today were not available. And, there was a fire in a St Louis building that destroyed military records.

Over 40 years after the war ended, he finally found a possible connection by hiring a private investigator promising he could find ANYONE. That connection was Bill Leek's Mother. He couldn't wait to call her. When she answered the phone, he got the answer he never could have imagined. Bill was there visiting his Mother for his annual visit. "Would you like to talk to Bill?" Mrs. Leek asked. Bill Leek brought his Pilot, his friend much happiness. Bill had been searching for his pilot. I think all of us would love to have a recording of that phone conversation. During that conversation, Bill Leek contradicted the accusatory letter from a former Macnab crew member that his pilot received after the war. "You saved my life. You did nothing wrong. You were not responsible for that collision." What relief for the Piggyback Flight Pilot. Bill also told Glenn the next 100th bomb group reunion was in Long Beach, California. Plans were made that day for the two pilots to reconnect at that 1987 reunion with some of the crew.

So happy to be together again were Herman Horencamp, Ed Neuhaus, Bill Leek, Glenn Rojohn, and Bob Washington.

Horenkamp, Neuhaus, Leek, Rojohn, Washington

Pilot and Co-Pilot are reunited as shown Glenn and Jane Rojohn with Bill and Marlene Leek

Bob and Nell Washington, Glenn and Jane Rojohn, Bill and Marleen Leek

Lt. Glenn H Rojohn was so excited to be at that reunion with his crew, his friends, that he taped the reunion meeting with Bill Leek right beside him like they were for 22 missions and for their time in Stalag Luft I.

That weekend in 1987, Lt. Glenn H Rojohn received another gift. He was an early riser. And there was 3 hour time difference between Pittsburgh and California. Ralph Christensen was also an early riser. The two of them were the first ones down from their rooms for coffee before dawn that first reunion meeting day. After brief introductions, Ralph recognized the name of the man he was meeting. Ralph told Glenn he witnessed the Piggyback Flight. He explained to The Little Skipper's pilot what happened. "I saw it" "It happened 50' off my right wing out my window." is always the way Ralph Christensen describes the collision. "You were not responsible. Nine Lives drifted up." Ralph Christensen had the best view. He was right next to the two planes as co-pilot of Lucky Lassie. The Lucky Lassie, Alternate Group Leader, didn't move out of position as the other planes were tightening up around them. The collision occurred of the right wing of the Lucky Lassie. Ralph had a front row seat. "Glenn H Rojohn, pilot of The Little Skipper was in position to go home. Unfortunately for him that did not happen."

The guilt and stress were gone. He could really enjoy reuniting with his crew, the men that made history together. Lt Glenn H. Rojohn's crew confirmed what Ralph Christensen had told him, he was not guilty as accused by one of Macnab's former crew member who was not part of the Piggyback Flight. They had always been grateful to their pilot and co-pilot for saving their lives that day. He was not guilty of what he was accused of over 40 years prior by one of Macnab's former crew members.

Glenn attended every reunion after the one in Long Beach, as did many of his crew. At the 1999 reunion in Cincinnati he received his Captain's bars that he had been awarded but not received.

Everyday after the 1987 reunion he proudly wore a cap signifying his war history. He was buried wearing his Century Bomber hat in his coffin.

Sadly Lt. Bill Leek only attended the first crew reunion. He died shortly after that Long Beach reunion. In late 2002 Glenn received a call in Florida from Pete Washington that his father, Bob, had just passed away. Glenn hung up saying to his family, "I am now the only one left of the Piggyback Flight."

When Captain Glenn H Rojohn was dying of untreatable melanoma in 2003, he was taking his final mission. He kept saying to his family, "I want to live long enough to go to Houston. I want to see that space shuttle operation. I want to see THAT instrument panel." Sadly, that was the life journey he didn't take.

CHAPTER 10

THE STORY IS REVEALED

Summer of 1988 was another time that changed Glenn H. Rojohn's life. The 100th Bomb Group reunion not only diminished the stress of his war experiences, but also renewed his interest in the B-17 flying fortress. He was very active in Mon Yough Chamber of Commerce and was able to be instrumental in bringing the Collings Foundation to Allegheny County Airport to display their war planes. His intention that day was to see the 909, shown, on display up close and personal. Glenn is pictured with his wife on the tarmac. No one could have predicted what happened on this day. Only a few people knew he was a legendary, historical bomber pilot. That situation changed very quickly. A 1988 summer day was the day his story became public. His days of a quiet uneventful retirement would be a memory not a reality.

Glenn and Jane Rojohn at Allegheny County Airport

Leonard and Glenn Rojohn at
Allegheny County Airport

He wore what would become his signature red, white and blue slacks and his Confederate Air Force B-17 Flying Fortress cap. All it took was a simple question about organizing the event and his cap. Quickly word spread among the attendees about December 31, 1944. It was a story that caught even his closest friends off guard as they had no clue about his war experiences. The two Rojohn Brothers, pictured with the 909, talked to the attendees and press about experiencing pilot training together. The stories about the Piggyback Flight and the two brothers training together were in multiple newspapers for the next few days as well as televised on local news stations. John Meredith and Glenn are holding the framed article from the Daily News in McKeesport, PA. On the second day of the event Lt. Rojohn was asked if he wanted to take a ride on the Flying Fortress. Rip Miere, close friend of Glenn's, said "I never, ever saw Glenn so excited." In addition to his ride over his hometown in the 909, Lt. Glenn H. Rojohn also rode in the 909 as part of the flyby that day waving to his family and the crowd. You could see him grinning from ear to ear.

John Meredith and Glenn with news clipping of event

The 1988 Allegheny County Air Show wasn't the only air show he attended telling his story and riding in his beloved ship. Sentimental Journey came to the Allegheny County Airport. He had met Ron Gorr thru the love of planes when he attended local flying organizations. Because Ron was trained to fly a B-17, he gave his friend a thrill of a life time--flying the B-17 again after forty plus years. Glenn was back in the pilot seat of a B-17 Flying Fortress. Lt. Glenn H. Rojohn also piloted the Fuddy Duddy at an Elmira, New York Air Show proudly wearing his 100th Bomb Group cap with Ron Gorr as his co-pilot. Not many veteran pilots are afforded that opportunity. Wonder how many times he looked to his right thinking of Bill Leek.

The 1988 Allegheny County Air Show was only the beginning of a flurry of activity. He found a new journey that would last through the rest of his life—education and dissemination of World War II historical information.

"You mean I'm going to pilot Sentimental Journey!"

Piloting the Fuddy Duddy

CHAPTER 11

LIFE CHANGING ACTIVITIES

Glenn H. Rojohn and his family had no idea a Chamber of Commerce event at Allegheny County Airport near Pittsburgh PA could change the Piggyback Flight Pilot's life. Because of that event a quiet retirement was not in his future.

The phone never stopped ringing. Mail was delivered to Lt. Rojohn almost daily. Friends, veterans, strangers, and news media wanted to be in touch. They wanted more information about the Piggyback Flight. Eyewitnesses wanted to relay their accounts. Reports arrived about the event of December 31, 1944. Some wanted to share their flying and/or war experiences. Organizations invited him to speak about his experiences. He experienced that activity until he no longer had the breath or energy to talk.

Eventually the VA became the source of Glenn's medical needs. The bomber pilot proudly wore one of his signature 100th Bomb Group caps. He met Veterans from all Wars each time he went. Some listened, others talked. The Vietnam Vets were the quiet ones because they just weren't ready to talk about their experiences. One day when they were gathered together they were approached by a freelance writer. Terry Flatley was looking for a story about Vietnam Veterans. Their response was "There is the guy you need to talk to." pointing to Lt. Rojohn. The result was "Breeding Dragon Flies over the North Sea" published in May 1997 WW2 magazine. A companion piece about the legend of the two brothers was also written. One of the cassette tapes that was found in 2015 was of Terry Flatley interviewing Glenn H. Rojohn for that story. The family was so appreciative of that tape as it answered many questions they needed answers to about the Piggyback Flight and the legend of the B-17 bomber pilot Brothers.

The Piggyback Flight Pilot was approached by Gregg Thompson about creating a painting of the legendary, historical collision. Rojohn, witness Ralph Christensen, and Navigator Bob Washington collaborated with Thompson to create The Piggyback Flight painting. The original painting has hung in the Mighty Eighth Air Force Museum in Pooler, Georgia and The Pentagon. In agreement with the artist, Washington, and Rojohn, 500 authenticated lithographs were produced to present to the crew members and to market at events. A portion of the proceeds of the sale of the prints went to various charities. One of the lithographs proudly hangs at Thorpe Abbotts.

Lithograph hanging at Thorpe Abbotts

Students from Butler Area School District in Pennsylvania interviewed veterans for a school project. Because of Rojohn's membership in the Western PA Wing 8th Air Force Historical Society and friendship with project developer Ralph A "Hap" Nicholas, he was one of the Veterans interviewed for the project. Teachers James Clements and Stephen Heasley and the students had a special request. "Could they use the picture of the Piggyback Flight on the cover of their book "Silent Heroes Among Us" to debut May 1997?" The book debut is shown with Glenn Rojohn at Butler Area High School. It was the perfect title to describe the crew members of the Piggyback Flight and World War II veterans.

A marriage of lithographs and books was the Glenn's new sales career and his true final mission. He and Jane traveled to air shows to sell the lithographs and books. They often traveled with Charles E Brewich, Fran Dugo, and Edith Brown pictured with Glenn and Jane. from the Western PA to local and east coast events. They wanted to share the veterans' experiences to anyone who wanted. to listen. The proceeds went to several organizations including the Golden Tornado Scholastic Foundation and 100th Bomb Group Foundation. Rojohn's favorite show was at the 911th Airlift Wing in Pittsburgh where he could talk to people from the Pittsburgh, PA area.

Charles Brewich, Fran Dugo, Edith Brown, Glenn, Jane

History was made at a Dayton Air Show in Ohio. Glenn and Jane were sitting at a table displaying the Piggyback Flight lithographs and "Silent Heroes Among Us". As the story is told, Glenn got up to mingle with the attendees. A man about his age casually asked him "Do you know anything about this Piggyback?" "I was the pilot." Rojohn answered. "My name is Grant Fuller, and I witnessed it." A forever friendship was formed that day. Grant was a 100th Bomb Group Foundation Board Member, but they had not met at any of the reunions. They spent time together at future reunions and corresponded regularly after that initial meeting.

In addition to "Silent Heroes Among Us" and The Story of the Century, the Piggyback Flight incident was described in several publications. A list of those publications can be found at the end of this chapter.

The requests from organizations for speeches kept coming. Since I am a Keynote Speaker, I suggested he do programs for large groups for a fee to supplement his Social Security. "I can't afford to do all that traveling." was his answer. "The organization would also pay for all your expenses." I replied. "You mean they would pay me and my expenses?" I nodded yes. "I could never let anyone pay for me to tell my story. That wouldn't be right." "And, I can't believe many people would want to hear me give a talk." he answered. He had no idea what a powerful message he had to tell. He had no idea how many audiences would want to hear him tell the story about the crews of the Piggyback Flight and the courage of The Little Skipper pilots and their crew. His family also would have loved to hear him give one of those speeches live. Unfortunately he always spoke during our work or school hours.

His favorite audience was an Elizabeth Forward Middle School program he as part of their Veteran's Day program. Marsha Cornell, 6th grade teacher, remembered those speeches. "Students had an instant connection and rapport with Captain Rojohn. He was like their grandfather. They never heard the word rutabagas. They were enamored with the word. You could hear a pin drop when he spoke." The students sent Captain Rojohn and his wife Thank You notes for coming to the program. They read every one and added them to their boxes of memorabilia. Rutabagas was the number 1 topic the students wrote about. Many asked him if he was scared during the Piggyback Flight and the time in prison camp. In an April 26, 2000 Post-Gazette article, Captain Rojohn talked about his speeches with students. "Sharing war stories with children--Think it is important to share with young people. All I had to eat the last three months was heavy black bread and rutabagas. Yes, several times I was scared. I was doing what my country asked me to do. Germans were doing what they were required to do."

The Piggyback Flight Pilot received many gifts. The Rojohn family wishes we knew who presented the Piggyback Flight Pilot with a gift that B-17 fans long for. The treasured B-17 model was something he treasured and proudly displayed in his family room.

Glenn H. Rojohn's illnesses took him to the VA facilities more frequently. They were very helpful when Glenn became ill in Florida. The VA hospital and staff knew the story by then. Because of their relationship, Captain Rojohn presented them with a lithograph of his legendary, historical event.

A devout Republican, Glenn H. Rojohn felt a sense of pride that President GW Bush sent him an autographed picture. After Captain Glenn H Rojohn's death, the family was sent a document honoring his service from Bush.

Elizabeth Township, the place his great, great grandfather came to raise his family and Glenn chose to raise his family, honored him at a Commissioners Meeting on June 2, 1997 for his service to his country and the legendary mission. The Commissioners accepted a lithograph from him. The lithograph would forever hang in the Commissioners Chambers as a display of life long resident's heroism. Pictured with the lithograph and proclamation are Jane Rojohn, Glenn, Commissioner Judy Marshall, Dave Rojohn, Cyndi Rojohn.

Rojohns with Commissioner Judy Marshall

Hall of Valor Induction Proclamation

His long time friend, Adam Lynch, nominated Captain Glenn H. Rojohn to be an honored inductee of the Soldiers & Sailors Hall of Valor in Pittsburgh. Notification of the induction is at the end of the chapter. Pictured is the proclamation presented that day. None of his family including him really knew what to expect on January 26, 2002. The room was filled with friends, supporters and military admirers. No one told him he had to give a speech. He was overwhelmed by the audience and the proclamation. He was so choked up with emotion that the speech was a difficult delivery. He did manage to say a few words. He was a man who rarely showed emotion. We remember the emotion he showed that day, none of the attendees remember what he said. Memories of that day: Glenn with the proclamation and Adam Lynch with Glenn. The Piggyback Flight Pilot donated mauser bayonet, Nazi armband, Wehrmacht belt buckle and breast patch, and Luffwaffe patches to the Soldiers & Sailors Memorial Hall. His family so wishes we had found a picture of these items in his collection.

An emotional Glenn with the proclamation

Nominator Adam Lynch with Glenn

Soldiers & Sailors Memorial Hall and Museum Trust, Inc.

Captain Glenn H. Rojohn
Hall of Valor Induction
January 26, 2002

Presentation of Colors ....Korean War Veterans
of Western PA

Invocation

Welcome...Joseph A Dugan, Jr.
President/CEO SSMH

Guest Host...Mr. Adam Lynch
8th Air Force Assn.

Remarks...Guests :
US Army Air Corps
8th Air Force Assn.
100th Bomb Group

Honoree...Mr. Glenn H. Rojohn

Closing Ceremony

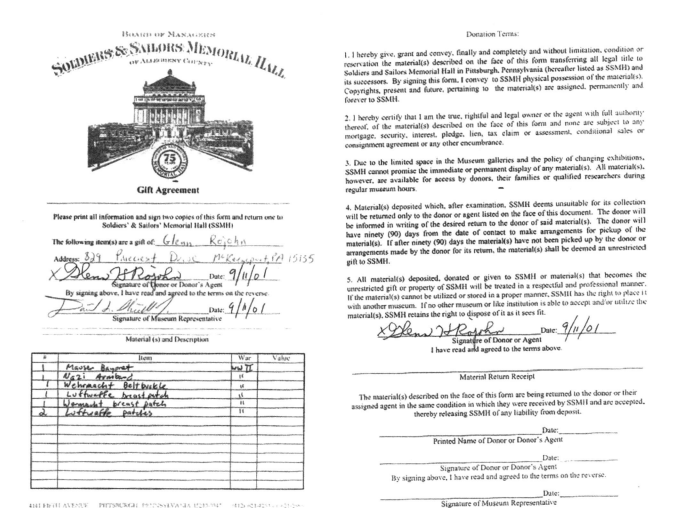

Glenn donated POW items to Soldiers & Sailors Memorial Hall

In 1997 he received a very important unexpected phone call. "Are you the Glenn Rojohn of the Piggyback incident?" the caller asked. The Lt. William Macnab family (MacNab or McNab in historical documents) knew their family member was killed in action, but did not know how. Gordon Hilderbrand was reading the article about the Piggyback incident in the WW2 magazine. He was the neighbor of the Macnab family. He couldn't get to the Macnab house fast enough. There it was in print, the account of what happened to their family member in World War II. Their long time question was answered. A mystery of war was solved. They wanted as much information as possible. So they decided to go to the source, the Piggyback Flight Pilot. That conversation resulted in a trip of a life time. A trip so Glenn and Jane Rojohn could meet the Macnab family to tell them the Piggyback Flight story in person was planned for May 1998 during that conversation. The trip was named Rojohn's Rendezvous.

Jane typed a journal upon their arrival back home documenting their activities. The following text is excerpts from that journal. Our family is so grateful she documented the meeting of the two families:

A tour of the Boeing Museum of Flight in Seattle was planned for the Rojohn and Macnab family as part of their visit. It was the company who manufactured his beloved flying fortress. A lithograph of the Piggyback Flight was sent by Glenn ahead of their visit, which still hangs in the museum. The Rojohns and Macnabs were given the royal tour. They also were given a royal tour of the Boeing Factory in Everett, Washington the next day. Everett, Washington was the childhood home of Bill Leek. (Lt. Leeks's memorabilia was donated to Lynden Pioneer Museum in Lynden, Washington by his sister.) The Piggyback Flight Pilot was one of the Grand Marshals in the Wasco Memorial Day Celebration. He presented the American flag to Mayor Elaine Kalista to fly over The Capitol by Senator Widen from Oregon in Lt. Bill Macnab's honor. Jane's complete typed journal of their trip can be found at the end of the chapter for you to read about their experience.

Adam Lynch and the Western Pennsylvania Wing 8th Air Force Historical Society brought him great joy a second time in his life. Unknown to Glenn or Jane or his family, there was not the usual program for one of their meetings. The event of the day was Gordon Hilderbrand and Macnab family members. Gordan Hilderbrand and the Macnabs flew in to thank Glenn for solving the mystery and saving members of Lt Bill Macnab's crew. They presented him with a plaque welcoming him as a family member. As the story is told there wasn't a dry eye at the meeting. A forever extended family was formed.

Glenn and Jane found four extended families—The 100th Bomb Group, Glenn's crew members, the Western Wing, and the Macnabs. The Long Beach reunion of the 100th Bomb Group created a bond that could really never be duplicated. As time grew shorter, the reunion to Houston kept him fighting his last fight. We knew he realized he couldn't fight the inevitable any longer when he said, "I guess I'm not going to make it to the Houston reunion."

Glenn with Macnab family and Gordan Hilderbrand

PUBLICATIONS REFERENCING THE PIGGYBACK FLIGHT

MAGAZINES

8TH AF NEWS March 2008
Ghost Wings Spring 2000 Volume 1, Issue 3
World War II May 1997
B-17 Flying Fortress Fall 2004

BOOKS

Contrails My War Record Contrails Publications
The Story of the Century John Nilsson editor
The Mighty Eighth A History of the US 8th Army Air Force
Roger A Freeman
Century Bombers the Story of the Bloody Hundredth
Richard Le Strange
Silent Heroes Among Us Golden Tornado Scholastic Foundation
Untold Until Now World War II Stories Karen Brantley

Prints in Glenn H. Rojohn Collection

The Piggyback Flight Gregg Thompson
Formidable Fortress Robert Bailey signed by Rojohn
Flying Fortress Boeing B-17
Confederate Air Force B-17 "Sentimental Journey"
Target Berlin March 4, 1944
Schweinfurt October 14, 1944
Beach Craft Army AT-10
Vultee Valiant US Army Navy Basic Trainer
Stearman PT-17 STOKES New Masters Gallery Carmel, CA

Rojohn's Rendezvous

This story begins in May of 1997 when Glenn received a call from Gordon Hilderbrand from Wasco, Oregon. He is a friend of the Macnab family.

Gordon read the article in the May issue of "World WII" Magazine about Glenn's Piggy-Back Story. He saw the name Macnab as the Pilot of the B17 (the bottom plane).

He told Glenn that the Macnab family had not known what happened to their brother until this article appeared. Glenn was able to send a lot of information about Bill Macnab (where he is buried, etc).

After a year of phone calls, letters, brochures they called and asked if we would come to Oregon to visit the family as their guests.

The following is a recount of our trip know as Rojohn's Rendezvous:

On May 19, 1998 Glenn and Jane left Pittsburgh International Airport via Chicago to Seattle, Washington to meet a group of 16 made up of relatives and friends of Bill Macnab. We went to the Hilton Inn where we were all staying overnight. After introductions and getting acquainted with everyone with being very emotional for all. We drove, in the van to the Thirteen Coins Restaurant for a very delicious lunch. Back in the van to visit the Boeing Museum of Flight.

Upon our arrival at the Museum there stood a newly refurbished B-17. Special arrangements were made as they knew this group was coming to visit and all were permitted to go through the plane. A reporter from Seattle KOMO TV Station interviewed the family and Glenn which appeared on the 11 o'clock news that evening. The group crossed the street and entered the Museum Building and there before our eyes was an easel with the lithograph that Glenn had sent in advance of our trip with a sign "Welcome Glenn Rojohn".

May 20 Th. we all got in the van to tour the Boeing Factory in Everett, Washington. Incidentally the home of Glenn's co-pilot. Bill Leek. We had been informed that most likely we wouldn't be able to go through the factory as tours had to be arranged ahead of time and due to summer vacations there would be many tourists, but we would be able to observe other activities. We arrived 20 minutes ahead of the 10:00 A.M. tour. Our tour director entered the building and explained Glenn's story plus the fact that we had traveled 3500 miles to go through the factory. The two employees were so fascinated they handed her the tickets for the whole group to take the 10:00 tour! We got to see the assembly line of 4 747's. Plus outside were many planes to be finished painting for various countries as ordered.

We left the factory and drove to Vancouver. Washington to the lovely home of Jean Macnab Witsburger (sister of Bill Macnab) for lunch. They dropped off Stuart. (Bills brother) in Portland. Oregon. Through the raindrops we saw the second largest rock formation (Beacon Rock) after the Rock of Gibraltar, Bonneville Dam. Bridge of the

Gods, which Lindbergh flew the Spirit of St. Louis under and arrive at The Dalles Shilo Inn for a week.

On Thursday we had a very interesting meeting with members of the "High Flyers Club" at the motel. All members attending told their individual stories and then Glenn related the Piggy Back Story. There was a period of questions and discussions and then the group had lunch. All knew Bill Macnab.

Then we went for a drive with Pete and Pat (cousins of Bill Macnab), Stuart and Gordon to see the acres of wheat farms around Wasco, Oregon. The Macnab family were and still are wheat farmers. On to visit the Sherman County Museum in Moro, which was most interesting.

On Friday the 22 nd. we were picked up by the Ericksons (friends) and went through the Oregon Cherry Growers cherry plant and the Northwest Aluminum Co. that makes stainless steel in The Dalles, plus the Historical Museum in The Dalles. Continued on after lunch to see the Erickson's Cherry orchard, went to their home to be interviewed by a newspaper reporter. *INCLUDED WAS A VISIT TO ROWENA LOOP WHERE SCENES IN "THE DEERSLAYER" WERE TAKEN.*
After all that we had been invited to another sister's home Anne Phillips, for dinner that evening.

Saturday we left for Mt. Hood at 10:30. Went to the Timberline Lodge, elevation 6,000 feet where it was snowing and blowing. This lodge was dedicated by Franklin D. Roosevelt in 1937. We had a very nice lunch in the restaurant. Quite and interesting place. The next day due to snow of 6 inches or more they closed the roads.

On the way back to The Dalles we toured the new Columbia Gorge Discovery Center - Wasco County Historical Museum. Quite nice and very modern.

Our plans for the evening: Glenn and I hosted a cocktail and hors d'oeuvre hour before dinner at the motel for a Macnab get-to-gather. We were told there might be a total of 20 people. Well! the member of the family, neighbors, and friends came out of the wheat fields, 71 people attended! Gifts to us were presented to our amazement.

On Sunday we were to go to Wasco for the afternoon. We visited the Railroad Depot, Masonic Lodge, Library, and several stores open. At 3 P.M. in the elementary school we attended a Buffet which honored the 3 Grand Marshals to appear in the parade Monday.

Glenn was one of the Grand Marshals at the Wasco Memorial Day Celebration and Centennial representing the armed services. Glenn presented the American flag to the Mayor (Elaine Kalista) that was flown over the Capitol by Sen. Widen from Oregon in Bills honor. He rode in a Model T Ford from the year 1916 in the parade.

Rojohn's Rendezvous

We had lunch at Tom Macnabs. a cousin after the parade. We looked at different exhibits in the town with Gordon. Wasco's population is 430. The parade lasted 1/2 hour including band, horses, vintage cars, nursery children on bikes.

Tuesday, our last day, we went to The Dalles Dam. the John Day Dam. both on the Columbia River hoping we could tour both of them, however, both were closed on Mondays and Tuesdays. We did get to go through parts of the Bonneville/Celilo Power Plant looking at exhibits showing the exchanges of AC - DC currents. We then crossed the Columbia River and went through the Maryhill Museum. Washington and Stonehedge a WWI Memorial.

Wednesday the 27 th. we were driven to Portland, Oregon airport by Pete and Pat Macnab and Gordon Hilderbrand to return to Pittsburgh.

It is very difficult to express the feeling and emotions we have plus the closeness with all these people we met on this "Rendezvous". Since we have come home we have received letters, telephone calls. photographs albums separate pictures, newspaper copies, 20 lbs. box of Bing Cherries (which are delicious). It was very hard to leave. They want us to return and perhaps someday in the future we may.

Glenn and I have been very fortunate to have had 2 wonderful trips, Germany and Washington and Oregon, all due to this crash. We have met so many nice people and have a lot of nice memories, pictures album and TV tapes. In a lot of ways it reminds you of our 100th. Bomb Group Reunions.

Rojohn's Rendezvous

CHAPTER 12

MR. GLENN RETURNS TO GERMANY

Glenn and Leonard at beach with Mother

Glenn H. Rojohn was a beach lover from the time he was a child. His parents frequently drove to Erie, PA where Glenn and Leonard could play in the sand and enjoy swimming with their mother and father. Therefore, it was not surprising that he vacationed at the beach with his children when they were growing up and during his retirement. When he bought 6 weeks in a Time Share in Lauderdale by the Sea, Florida in 1981, he never could have imagined it would eventually be connected to his life as a pilot. During his 20 years there he found a new journey and another extended family. He created a competitive game with himself and Native Sun Resort time-share residents called "the best shell catch of the day" game. He did not like to lose. He and Jane spent hours on the beach where Glenn could show off his prized catch of the day to his friends and people on the beach.

Who would believe time on the beach for the Piggyback Flight Pilot would give closure for the December 31, 1944 collision over the North Sea near the Island of Wangerooge and Tettens Field?

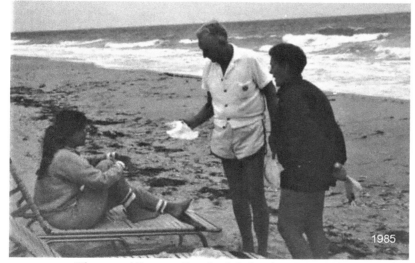

1985

Glenn and Jane on Lauderdale by the Sea Beach

Hans Jurgen Juergens was in the process of writing the history of Wangerooge. The Piggyback Flight was a part of the island's history. The only name they knew was Ed Neuhaus. His parachute took him to land on Wangerooge. Believe it or not, Sgt Neuhaus was invited to join German soldiers for a New Year's Eve dinner while waiting for directives from German officials. Thankfully those Germans learned and remembered his name.

Hans Jurgen Jurgens contacted several United States agencies before locating Ed Neuhaus. He sent Ed a letter searching for information on the

Piggyback Flight and crew members. The letter was written in German so Ed couldn't read it. Ed decided to send the letter to his Pilot, his friend who had it translated. The translated letter is at the end of the chapter for

you to read. The story Rojohn tells is that he carried that folded letter in his wallet just so he could read story to tell himself that what happened in the air over the North Sea was truly real.

In the fall of 1995, a German tourist by the name of Freddie Feix was vacationing in the USA. His Florida stop was at The Native Sun in Lauderdale by the Sea. One day when he stopped in the resort's office, he noticed the lithograph of two B-17 planes flying hooked together. Freddie was a German fighter pilot. He was very familiar with the incident over the North Sea. He asked the office staff "Does anyone know anything about this?" He was told "The pilot is the President of the Condo Association." "How can I contact this man?" Freddie asked. He was told "You could probably find him shelling on the beach." The Piggyback Flight Pilot and the German fighter pilot became instant friends. Any animosity of the war between their countries had disappeared long ago. Freddie couldn't wait to tell his home country he had found the Piggyback Flight Pilot. Faxes were sent back

Fred Feix
Fighter Pilot Luftwaffe WWII August 1942

and forth to Germany during that vacation. Hans Juergen Juergens and the Piggyback Flight Pilot made an important connection. Because of that connection, Rudolf Skawran was able to correspond with Glenn to share his recollection of December 31, 1944 which is included in the documents at the end of the chapter.

Freddie and Glenn spent many vacations together in Florida. During one of those vacations, Glenn presented Jack Berkowitz, Navigator of Macnab's crew, with a lithograph. Jack told him his pilots were dead slumped in their seats.

In 1996, Piggyback Flight Pilot Glenn H. Rojohn received an invitation to go on a trip he never would have thought possible. The invitation was to travel back to Germany to the site of the Piggyback Flight landing. Glenn mentioned in several conversations that he had gone to Germany on business trips but never thought of visiting the crash site.

Glenn, Jack, Freddie

Glenn shows Jack a lithograph

Aviation friends Mitch Cowan and Jordan Brown made that trip happen for the Rojohns. The US Air Pilots gave Glenn and Jane Rojohn buddy passes so they could take the trip. Freddie Feix and Hans Juergen Juergen made all the arrangements for the historical visit.

On September 6, 1996 Glenn H. Rojohn and his wife started their journey to Germany where the Piggyback Flight Pilot made history. The Rojohns had a brief stay with Freddy and Geddy Feix. Then the four of them traveled to where it all happened.

The first stop was to have lunch with Bruno Albers and his wife Hanna. Bruno, was not only a witness but he was in the Operation Center when the incident over the North Sea occurred. Glenn and Jane reviewed the silk escape maps that are part of his memorabilia collection. Glenn wanted to remember what the land looked like and the mission path in 1944 so he had something to prepare him for what he would see on this journey.

Glenn with Albers in Germany

Jane and Glenn viewing his silk maps

Unknown to the Rojohns, Bruno had made arrangements for the other Piggyback Flight witnesses to meet the legendary pilot. They gathered with a TV Camera Team Der Norddeutsche Rundfunk, a Northern German TV-Station, to film the activities scheduled for that day.

Glenn with German witnesses

Glenn with TV crew

The Rojohns had no knowledge of any of the activities planned for their trip. Another surprise for them was a flight that would take them on the same route Rojohn and Leek took in The Little Skipper with Nine Lives hooked underneath them decades earlier. It was a gift from the people of Wangerooge. Mr. Kipp was the pilot. They flew to the sight of the collision over the North Sea. Then flew across the Island of Wangerooge where Neuhaus landed. Lt. Rojohn no longer needed a letter to tell him December 31, 1944 was real,

Glenn over Piggyback Flight path

Piggyback Flight path map

HE WAS RELIVING IT. The scenery was different than it was December 31, 1944. They were crossing green fields instead of barren, frozen territory filled with landmines. Bruno had mapped out the flight path to get ready for the historic pilot's visit. When the small plane carrying Piggyback Flight Pilot neared the landing site, Bruno announced "This is the spot". All Rojohn and Leek remembered was hitting ground as drawn by Bruno Albers, a building, coming to a stop, and realizing they were alive.

Field where they landed

The landing by Bruno Albers

The next stop for everyone was to visit the landing spot. Bruno presented Captain Glenn H. Rojohn with his drawing of the landing. Now it was time for the Piggyback flight Pilot to stand alone on the historical sight. Lots of tears and smiles occurred that day. Glenn and Jane Rojohn had met new friends that were part of Glenn's life 52 years before.

Bruno investigated "Mr. Glenn's" crash-landing-meadow...

..and showed everybody the site

Glenn standing on the spot where they landed

Sometime during their trip back to revisit the Piggyback Flight, Glenn H. Rojohn received a gift. The boy who retrieved his military pistol from the field where Glenn had tossed it gave the pistol back to him. The pistol is now stored in a box at The Mighty Eighth Museum in Pooler, Georgia.

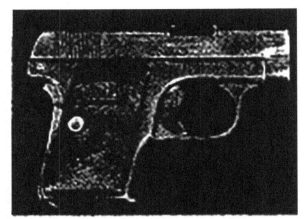

This Colt .25 Caliber Automatic Pistol, manufactured in late 1919, was Glenn Rojohn's personal side arm. David Graham recently donated it to the Museum.

The next day they were going to visit the Island of Wangerooge where Ed Neuhaus landed. As they were landing Glenn remarked, "Look at all the American flags. President Clinton must be visiting, Glenn exclaims pointing to the flag on the tower". As they entered the Town Hall, it soon became clear the flags were flying honoring the Piggyback Flight. The Town Hall was filled with American flags and a huge sign that read WELCOME BACK MR. GLENN.

Control tower flying welcome flag

Pictured are Geddy Feix, Glenn, the town Mayor, Jane, Freddie. Mr Juergens described that moment, "Everybody now wants to meet 'The Pilot—Mr Glenn Rojohn', a man they talked about over the years and years and nobody knew what you looked like, now they do." Sadly it was time to leave his new German friends involved with the legendary, historic Piggyback Flight. Hans Jurgen Juergens and the trip's pilot, Mr. Kipp presented the Piggyback Flight Pilot with the American flag that flew on the tower.

Rojohns and Feix with Wangerooge Mayor

Hans and Mr Kipp present the flag to Glenn H Rojohn

Jane and Glenn stayed in Germany a few more days with their friends Freddie and Geddi Feix. They needed time to reflect on the past days activities, celebrate the previous days journey, and find time for a little sight seeing. In a speech he gave in Pleasant Hills, PA., Glenn told the audience that he received another surprise on his trip back to Germany. Glenn found the church where his great, great grandfather was baptized in the 1800s.

Glenn's family church

Scrapbook of Rojohn's Germany Trip

The Rojohn family is so grateful to those who documented the trip in a scrapbook so we could better understand what happened during their visit.

For Captain Glenn H. Rojohn, this trip back to Germany was the highlight of his life. He talked about the visit back to Germany. But not the emotions he was feeling. He was a man of few words and rarely showed emotion.

Glenn H. Rojohn was born and raised on a farm in a small town near Pittsburgh PA. He made history twice on a farm field in his families homeland. The Piggyback Flight Pilot's twilight years were approaching quickly. It was as if he needed to take that journey and stand on that field one more time for his life to be complete.

Hans-Jürgen Jürgens
Carstens-Straße 22

26486 Wangerooge

Wangerooge, den 9.12.1994

Dr. Edward G. Neuhaus
4236 Rugby Drive

Toledo, Ohio 43614

Dear Dr. Neuhaus,

       I received your address from the German Embassy
in Washington, and I am glad that I finally found you and your
relatives.
As the author of the "War Diary" that you will get by air-mail
today, I have always kept in my head this extraordinary story
which had happened half a century ago on this New Year's Eve.
As a young pilot you had been lucky that you were able to save
your life on that 31 st of December 1944 while many young people
of the two crews had to die.
You will know whether such a situation of two four-engine bombers
being so closely wedged had occurred a second time in this war.
With us here it was a special and mysterious occurrence which
had been observed and watched by a few thousand people on the
shore. A woman from further inland told me by phone:"This story
is thought of in our family every New Year's Eve".
You probably ask yourself why I have searched for you. For one,
in three weeks' time it will be half a century ago that you could
celebrate an extra birthday. On the other hand I found the gesture
of the German soldiers who took you out of the detention room good.
(Today this building serves as school building of the island).
Moreover, now, after 50 years, there are no resentments left between Americans and Germans.
I have experienced that there were much less problems between soldiers of both sides, also between Germans and forced laborors of
the older generation than sometimes between young people who get
to know the history of those times only through the media.
Then, of course, I am interested to know what the further course
of your war experiences were and when you finally returned home.

Letter to Ed Neuhaus from Jurgens

- 2 -

In our country such stories are occasionally told on TV, but
I assume it will be too late for that, because time has elapsed.
I have been trying to find your address in various ways for near-
ly one year.

By the research work I did for my book I got to know a former
navy soldier who had sat with you at a party on New Year's Eve
in 1944. Then I also know a lady, a former navy assistent, who
watched you coming down by parachute among the heavy anti-aircraft fire that went into the sky, and you were taking off your
boots in the air. You must have feared to be drifted away by parachute into the sea.

Finally, I received a letter from Pretoria, South Africa, today.
It is from Rudolf Skawran, a former navy assistant, who lives
there und who also describes your parachute jump inmidst the
anti-aircraft fire in his War Diary. Perhaps you could send him
greetings, he will certainly appreciate it. Since he speaks English there, there will be no language barrier. You see that your
story is still alive among the older generation.

You will certainly hear something again from here. For today
I send you my best wishes from Wangeroode together with greetings
for Christmas and New Year.

             Yours

                  gez. Hans-Jürgen Jürgens

             page 2

Mr.Glenn H. Rojohn   From:R.F.Skawran
829 Pine Crest Avenue   70 Cecilia Road
MC KEESPORT,PA 15135   0181 Maroelana-PRETORIA

                                                 16/1/96

Dear Glenn!

It was absolutely thrilling to hear from Hans-Jürgen Jürgens that he had succeeded
at long last to establish contact with not only one of the crew members of the two
Fortresses flying 'stuck together' over our gun battery in Wangerooge on 31/12/44,
but indeed with the pilot who had succeeded to land the two planes! Hans-Jürgen
phoned me immediately after his telephone conversation with you and Mr.Feix and
also sent me copies of the various faxes transmitted between Florida and Wangerooge.
What a pleasant surprise this all was and how fascinating it was to read about your
experiences on that memorable day.The way this contact came into being was an
equally interesting story,full of chance factors. – What did the boy of the US TV pro-
gramme 'The A-Team' always say?Wasn't it 'I.love it when a plan comes together!!!?
I certainly agree with this fullheartedly!!! – Hans-Jürgen then suggested that I
write to you personally and I gladly do so!
Since you probably would like to know who I am and how I fit into this story,here
are a few details which will hopefully help you to form a picture.– I was drafted
into the German Navy at the end of 1943 and posted to serve in the heavy anti-
aircraft gun battery (105 mm) Neudeich on Wangerooge. There I served as an operator
on the optical rangefinder until the end of the war.–In 1948 I was able to return
to South Africa (where I was born).Initially I landed a job with the South African
Meteorological Services,amongst others serving for a year on Marion Island (close
to the Antarctic!).On completion of my parttime studies I joined the National
Institute for Personnel Research as a psychologist.In this capacity I had a lot
to do with military selection issues,therefor also the selection of pilots.(In-
terestingly enough,the selection of German fighter pilots was also my father's
job as a psychologist during the war!).I retired in 1993,at the time as Director
of the institute.
My contact with Hans-Jürgen also came about by chance.Somebody wrote a book about
us youngsters serving in the anti-aircraft gun batteries during the war.Some of
his facts about the bomber atttack by the RAF on us on 25/4/45 were wrong and I
wrote to him about this.He had,however,no further interest in the matter and forwarded my letter to Hans-Jürgen,knowing that the latter was busy writing a book
on Wangerooge during the war.Hans-jürgen immediately wrote to me,bombarding me

Skwaran letter

2

with questions about my experiences on Wangerooge,knowing that I had kept a diary during
that time.A lively correspondence developed and it was during this time that I wrote
to him about the events on 31/12/44!What I wrote to him about your epic flight (as well
as many other episodes) he included in his book on page 517.I believe you have a copy
of it in your possession - a very interesting and valuable book indeed!My wife and I
visited him in 1988 and we have been in regular contact with him ever since.
I do remember the events of 31 December 1944 quite clearly.Your piloting feat with those
two Fortresses on that day must be truly unique in the annals of the war and was absolutely outstanding!Unfortunately I was not one of those privilaged to see with their
own eyes what was happening outside,most of us being fully engaged in the gun- or rangefinder turrets.Only the batterychief (Oberleutnant Brodbeck,page 408),the firing leader
(Feldwebel Ahrends) and the Sergeant-Major Hildebrand (who,incidently,was the one who
'captured' Neuhaus - pages 408,176) as well as the three operators of the rangefinder
(elevation,side and range) could see what was happening.The guy who had to measure the
range with his powerful 40 x glasses was the luckiest of them all.He was sitting close
to me,and where normally you only heard the respective distances,etc.,being called out
and nothing else was heard,I remember very clearly the disbelief and excitement when
Obergefreiter Müller spotted the two Fortresses locked together,providing us with a
running commentary,ending when your crew started parachuting out of the planes.From
that moment on we switched to new targets.The next surprise came when Neuhaus came
floating by,amidst the shell trajectories of the shooting guns (aiming at a Liberator)
and landing safely behind our battery on the heavily mined airfield. - How lucky he
was not to trigger off one of the mines.I know this,because I was one of those who,once
the war was over,was designated to clear the mines on the airfield (which by then was
ploughed by bombs during the bomber attack of 25/4/45).Apart from the so-called T-mines
there were also the vicious and highly sensitive anti-personnel mines!!
The events of the day,such as the shooting down of a Liberator,but above all the two
Fortresses locked together in flight and flying,were discussed at length.-It was only
much later,i.e. during the course of my correspondence with Hans-Jürgen,that I got to
know where you managed to land the plane.You can imagine how pleased I was when I heard
that you had survived!!Naturally I am curious about what happened to you afterwards,
e.g. where you were taken to and when you were able to return to the USA!
Hans-Jürgen sent me a fax picture of the painting of that memorable flight.I studied
it,naturally with keen interest,touching up the poor fax copy where necessary to get
the planes standing out more clearly.Would it be possible for you to take a colour
photograph of this painting and send me a photo print of it?!I hope you will understand
my request and forgive me for being so immodest?! - Looking at the painting I was
rather intrigued by the fact that all usual exits must have been effectively blocked
by the lower plane.How did your crew manage to bale out and,what is more,in doing so,
how did they manage to fall free without hitting the other Fortress? It is also not
clear from the picture how many engines of the lower plane were still running?!
If one considers all the information available about this amazing incident,one naturally
wonders whether this was ever written down in the form of a small book,an article,etc.,
similar to the film on the 'Memphis Belle'? I do feel that this is morethan warranted!!

I hope that you are well and may I use this occasion,even if it is a little late,to
wish you everything of the best for 1996!Good health in particular!! - I do hope that
you will find a little time to drop me a line or two.If there is anything you would
like to know,please do not hesitate to write to me!
Kindest regards

Rudolf

page 2

Pretoria, 26/2/96

Dear Glenn!

Thank you most sincerely for your letter and the excellent copy of your outstanding painting! I was thrilled to receive them both so soon after I had written to you!
I would also like to thank you for filling me in on some of the details concerning your memorable flight. In this regard the painting done by Thompson (?) was outstanding and is really magnificent, both artistically and in terms of technical detail! It certainly helps to picture what happened.
Two days before your letter arrived, I received the letter sent by Fred Foix from Florida. His letter, written on the 10th of December, therefor took more than two months to reach me! I have already replied, but I thought it best to phone him as well. Just as well that I did, because he may be on his way to America before my letter arrives. - He was understandably surprised to receive a call from Pretoria! What a nice chat we had! - During the course of our conversation he told me that you already had sent him a copy of my letter. He was also in possession of an article Hans-Jürgen had sent him and he intends to send you a copy of this well-written article when he is in Las Vegas.
I have been thinking about some of the details which might be of interest to you to supplement the information

Skwaran documentation

you already have. In this regard I thought it best to refer you to certain pictures, etc., in the book of Hans-Jürgen. As you know, his book is so comprehensive that it is not so easy to find very specific details of personal interest to you, i.e. unless you are able to read German and have studied all the details. — In my previous letter I already started to indicate to you some of the pictures which would be of specific interest to you. Reflecting on this I discovered a few others which might be of value to you. They are briefly the following:

* <u>105 mm Guns of the Battery Neudeich</u>
The best pictures of these heavy anti-aircraft guns within their camouflaged steel turrets are on pages 245 (normal weather), 529 (in winter) and 487 (at night).

* <u>Rangefinder of the Battery Neudeich</u>
This rangefinder was also known as Kommandogerät 36 and directed the fire of all the guns (firing every five seconds in salvos). It was also housed under a steel turret. As you already know, this is where I served as an operator (these were ten of us in the team). On page 594 you see the inside (and also saw it from my position!) and the operator you see in the picture is the guy who does the range measuring (and saw you first!). On page 636 you get an idea as to how it looked from the outside. Concerning the rangefinder during your flight, I wrote in my previous letter that the rangefinder's name was Obergefreiter Müller. I made a mistake, his name was actually Obergefreiter Heinrich Brinkmann. He was killed in action 1 d. in the RAF attack on us.

Page 2

" Battery Neudeich

You will find a diagrammatic layout of the battery on page 602. I am sure that you would like to know how the battery looked like from the air, i.e. as you might have seen it (given a chance from your position on that day). In this regard the two reconnaissance pictures on pages 540 and 541, taken on 24/2/45 at a height of 7200 m, provide the answer. It is the picture on page 540 which is the better one for finding the batte. Let me help you by means of a sketch. You will also need an enlarging glass to discover the five turrets (4 for the guns and 1 for the rangefinder, ⊙▽⊙ / ⊙ ⊙).

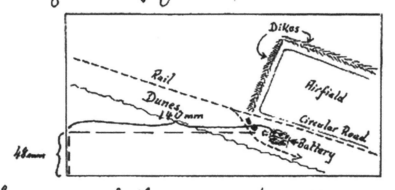

If you use a ruler the measurements are 48 mm up and 140 mm to the right. – Enjoy the spotting exercise !!
Let me end my letter today with two other memories of that time. –
The first one relates to the first experiences with the 'Flying Fortresses'.
As you know, the Germans were pretty much awed when these planes entered the war. For the fighters they were a serious problem until they resorted to the frontal attack strategy. But also for the anti-aircraft gunnery the question arose whether such planes could be shot down effectively with the normal time-fused shells.

Page 3

4

There was a time when we were told not to shoot at Fortresses with the latter, but to use shells which exploded on impact only!! – The appearance of the huge US bomber formations during daylight was indeed awe-inspiring. I remember (and I noted this in my diary) that on one occasion we ventured to count the planes passing us. At 1200 we gave up, because the first ones had disappeared behind the one horizon when the last ones had not yet appeared over the other horizon!! I do not think that this sort of sight of an air-armada will ever be seen again!

Well Glenn, I do hope you found some of the information in this letter of interest to you. – I would be grateful to hear from you again. Please do not worry about the 'typing issue.' I could read your letter without any difficulties. I also hate to use a type-writer. It is a time-consuming business to correct your mistakes as you go along!

Stay well! The heartiest greetings from South Africa!

Kindest regards

Rudolf.

CHAPTER 13

DEATH OF A LEGEND

On August 9, 2003 Captain Glenn H. Rojohn lost his battle with melanoma. Obituary from the Tribune Review is pictured below. The last crew member of the Piggyback Flight joined The Little Skipper and Nine Lives crew members flying high above the clouds. He was honored by POW ceremony and a missing man squadron over the cemetery where he would be buried with his family. His family cried when they received the honorary flag that draped his coffin.

WWII pilot's resiliency served him at war, in life

By Dan Reynolds
TRIBUNE REVIEW

Glenn Rojohn

Glenn Rojohn never thought of himself as a hero, but he might have pulled off one of the most amazing flying feats in military history.

The McKeesport native crash-landed two B-17 bombers that became stuck together — his on top — after flying a bombing mission over Germany on New Year's Eve 1944. He was awarded the Air Medal, Distinguished Flying Cross and Purple Heart.

Glenn Rojohn, 81, of the Elizabeth Township, Allegheny County, village of Greenock, died Saturday, Aug. 9, 2003, at his home.

He was born April 6, 1922, in Greenock, the son of the late Harry and Selma Benlhausen Rojohn.

The resilient spirit that kept Mr. Rojohn going during the harrowing moments of what is known as the "Piggyback Flight" was evident in his last days, his wife, Jane, said.

"Well, I'll tell you what I found out about him in the last couple of days ... he was a fighter like I never knew, he was fighting for his breath and his life," she said.

While he talked little about it to family and friends, Mr. Rojohn's epic flight was more than a remarkable feat. It saved lives.

A second lieutenant in the 100th Bomb Group, Mr. Rojohn and his fellow pilots flew a mission Dec. 31, 1944, during the Battle of the Bulge, to attack Hamburg, Germany — home to oil refineries and submarine pens.

The 31 aircraft encountered heavy flak and wave after wave of attacks from German fighter planes. Twenty-five planes made it back.

As Mr. Rojohn and another B-17 pilot, 1st Lt. William McNabb, maneuvered their planes to fill a gap in their formation, the aircraft melded together. A propeller from Mr. Rojohn's plane lodged in one of McNabb's engines, sparking a fire, and McNabb's turret guns pierced the belly of Mr. Rojohn's plane, locking the aircraft together.

With other pilots in the formation watching in horror, Mr. Rojohn cut his engines. As the engines on McNabb's plane whirred on, Mr. Rojohn and copilot Lt. Bill Leek wrestled the controls in an effort to save the planes' crews.

Crew members bailed out shortly before the planes came crashing to the earth near Wilhelmshaven, Germany. McNabb's exploding on impact and Mr. Rojohn's sliding off and skidding across the ground, a wing slicing through a wooden headquarters building.

Three crew members from each plane who made it out before the crash survived. All were captured by Germans. Mr. Rojohn spent five months as a POW.

If either Mr. Rojohn or Leek, who also survived the crash landing, had relinquished the controls, the planes would have crashed into the frigid ocean.

"It's a good thing that we were stronger then than I am now," Mr. Rojohn told the Tribune-Review in January 2002, when he was inducted into the Hall of Valor of the Soldiers & Sailors Hall in Pittsburgh's Oakland section.

Mr. Rojohn was the last surviving member of the famous flight. His navigator, 2nd Lt. Robert Washington, died in 2002, Jane Rojohn said yesterday.

Mr. Rojohn's son, David, 50, of West Mifflin, Allegheny County, said his father never mentioned the heroics until about 10 years ago.

David Rojohn said he and his sister, Cyndi, never were allowed to watch war movies, and the family never celebrated New Year's Eve — the anniversary of the "Piggyback Flight."

David Rojohn said his understanding of his father's achievement has deepened with time.

"I'm a civil engineer and I understand physics, and it's just amazing that anybody survived," he said.

Mr. Rojohn is survived by his wife, Jane; son, David G., of West Mifflin, and daughter, Cynthia, of Elizabeth Township; brother, Leonard E., of Mt. Vernon, Chester County; and grandchildren, nieces and nephews.

Friends will be received from 2 to 4 and 7 to 9 p.m. today and Tuesday at Gilbert Funeral Home, Boston, Allegheny County, where a service will be held at 10 a.m. Wednesday with the Rev. Andrew Wahl and the Rev. David S. Lake officiating. Interment will follow at Peace Lutheran Cemetery, Greenock.

Memorial contributions may be made in honor of Mr. Rojohn's grandson Nathan to The Children's Institute, 6301 Northumberland St., Pittsburgh, PA 18213-3547 or Three Rivers Hospice, 3001 Jacks Run Road, White Oak, PA 15131.

Dan Reynolds can be reached at dreynolds@tribweb.com or 412-380-8533.

KDKA TV in Pittsburgh aired a segment on his death reported by Ross Guidotti which included interviews with Glenn's children. It complimented a piece he aired interviewing Captain Glenn H. Rojohn as part of a series on rapid declining numbers of The Greatest Generation. Fox News in Pittsburgh, PA also aired a piece on Rojohn's death and the Piggyback Flight.

As history would have it, the most important tribute written about the death of the Piggyback Flight Pilot was written by Ralph Kinney Bennett. His article titled "Brave Heart" or sometimes called "Piggyback Hero". Why was it the most important you ask? The obituary with the picture of Gregg Thompson's painted image has gone viral over and over. One posting posting of the story and the painting on Facebook had 10,000 hits. The story of the legendary, historical Piggyback Flight will live forever for generations to come.

The Piggyback Flight Pilot is shown with his head bowed standing on site of crash.

Tettens..

..this is the place

Captain Glenn H. Rojohn's life ended in 2003. One would think that was the end of the journey. For his family the journey just started.

CHAPTER 14

THE NEXT GENERATION'S JOURNEY

A phone conversation in February 2014 nudged Captain Rojohn's family to focus on the Piggyback Flight. After Jane McCormick Rojohn's sudden death in 2009, the family found boxes and boxes of World War II and Piggyback Flight documents, pictures, and memorabilia. When their mother died they sorted through what was in the house but not what was in those boxes. That phone call in February 2014 made it clear the family needed to know exactly what those boxes held.

They also knew they needed to contact the other families. Fortunately they were blessed with Jane's address book. In three days I had talked with the majority of the Piggyback Flight Families.

So honored I was able to talk with Herman Horenkamp and his wife Pauline. We all remembered their visit to Glenn and Jane's home decades before. He was pleased we had all the documentation of the wartime experiences. At the time of this writing both Horenkamps were alive. Each time I called I could tell they were fading a little more.

My most memorable call was to Pearl Neuhaus. She answered "Why are you calling me?" I assumed she thought I was a telemarketer. I told her who I was. "I know who you are. Why are you calling me?" She replied. A new friendship was born. She knew nothing about the Piggyback Flight but couldn't wait for me to tell her all the details. She talked with much sadness that her children threw out all the War Memorabilia and regret she wasn't able to attend all the reunions with Ed. Tears filled my eyes when her son told me the following year that she joined the crew in Heaven.

Edith Berkowitz, wife of Jack Berkowitz, was alive and doing well. I have talked to her the most over the years, filling her in on the progress of our projects. Like all of us, she knew little about what happened December 31, 1944.

That February 2014 phone conversation also nudged us to create websites www.piggybackflight.com and www.breedingdragonflies.com plus Facebook page Piggyback Flight. We also copyrighted a synopsis of Glenn's experience that includes a voice recording of one of his Piggyback Flight speeches. Now we were on our own Piggyback Flight journey. We wanted to protect the history of the legendary flight and tell the story of what happened December 31, 1944.

New to Facebook, I was not aware the format on most World War II pages was to submit a bio of your relationship to each specific group. I was immediately accepted on the sites without a bio that I signed on to join. What an honor to Glenn H Rojohn that no one asked. They knew the name and the story. I remember finding and joining WW2 100th Bomb Group page. I was on a new search for Piggyback Flight crew families. I was immediately greeted by Mike Faley. "You must be related to Glenn Rojohn". That was the beginning of our relationship with the 100th Bomb Group Foundation. I was still on a search for family members. Bill Leek's daughter, Kim, was the first one I found on that Facebook page. Over the years I was able to find families through Facebook, or they found the Piggyback Flight page. Fortunately thousands of people are learning the image of two B-17s flying together over the North Sea is real not a photo shop. I was proud to interact with people about the legendary, historical flight.

Rojohn family with the collection

The 70th Anniversary of the Piggyback Flight was celebrated by the family telling the story in the local paper that carried the Piggyback Flight story the first time it was told—The Daily News in McKeesport, PA. We wanted to showcase a sample of the memorabilia we found in our parents house. Pictured are Cyndi, Gavin and Dave Rojohn. Proclamations from the Senate of Pennsylvania and one from Allegheny County in western Pennsylvania marking the anniversary were among the pictured items. The article was written by Carol Waterloo Frazier, one of my former students.

Volker Urbansky at crash site

Through Facebook, I was able to connect with two important people who were involved with the Piggyback Flight story. The Piggyback Flight families are grateful to Volker Urbansky who found the crash site near the former Tettens Field. During that find he was able to find remnants of Nine Lives. Shown are bullets and plane remnants The Piggyback Flight families are also grateful to Ferry Harreman who adopted the gravesite of Lt. William Macnab at Margarten in the Netherlands. He is pictured with Bo Macnab, cousin of Bill's, and his wife Mary.

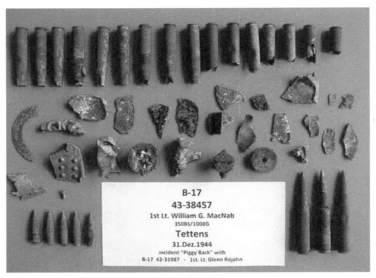

Discovered remnants

Bo Macnab, Ferry Harreman, Mary Macnab

Also because of Facebook we were sent the picture of the street sign that was erected prior to 2012 as part of the RAF Mildenhall refurbishing project. The sign to honor the Piggyback Flight was the idea of Nolan Vujevic and Jeff Lehnert.

At RAF Mildenhall

The Elizabeth, PA Area started a military banner program to display the pictures of residents who served their country. The banners will be displayed from Memorial Day to Veterans Day every year starting in 2016. Now the Piggyback Flight Pilot will be proudly displayed not only in the Municipal Building but along the roadway for everyone to see.

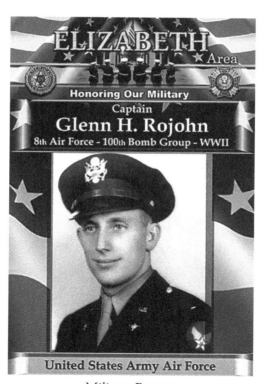

Military Banner

September 2015 I attended the 100th Bomb Group Reunion in New Orleans. It was my first time to attend. It was also the first time anyone from the Piggyback Flight attended since 2005. I was overwhelmed by the questions and interest in the Piggyback Flight. The reason I went to the reunion was to acquire more information about the legendary flight. I soon found out the attendees wanted information from me, and at that time I didn't know all the answers. Thanks to Brandon Andersen, who I met on Facebook, they could easily find me because of the T-shirt he made for the Rojohn family members. I was proud to wear one of Captain Rojohn's signature 100th Bomb Group caps with his treasured pins.

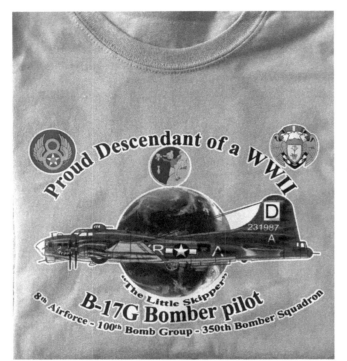

Brandon Andersen created T-shirts for the Rojohn family

My favorite part of the reunion was sitting in a lobby area having an impromptu discussion about the Piggyback Flight. Board Treasurer Dave Distelrath and his wife were asking Ralph Christensen and me questions. It was a lively 30 minute discussion. When I got home I felt so much regret that the conversation wasn't taped to add to ours and the 100th Bomb Group's collection.

What a wonderful experience meeting Piggyback Flight witness Ralph Christensen and Roy Little's family Rich and Joanne Hehn. I also met many of the members I had talked with on Facebook the past year. I also had the honor of spending time with Mike Miller, son of Ray Miller. Ray Miller was the piece of the puzzle I couldn't find in my Mother's directory. He was one my Father's closest friend in the 100th Bomb Group. I am honored I was able to talk with him before he died shortly after our conversation. I wish he had lived long enough to read this book that honors his friend.

Ralph Christensen with Cyndi, Joanne and Rich Hehn

I realized why my parents couldn't wait to attend every reunion. The 100th Bomb Group is a forever family. I understand that now. I didn't when I attended the opening of the 100th Bomb Group Restaurant in Cleveland in 2003 with my mother right after my Father's death. As a man passed me in the hall of the restaurant, he commented "I saw it I was a witness". At the time it didn't register what he meant. I now know that was Hong Kong Wilson. A missed opportunity to talk with him I will always regret. Later my brother and I were in contact with his son, Curtis.

I remember when we entered the dining room my mother saying "Rosie wants us to sit with him!" in an excited voice. I was glad we had people to sit with that she knew. I was sitting next to this kind gentle man who was talking about Captain Glenn H. Rojohn, the Piggyback Flight legend and how grateful he was that I brought my Mother to the event. I was too embarrassed to say "Sir, I really don't know the story because my father didn't talk about it." Many of those reading this may know who my dinner partner was. What I would do to have that moment back. I would love to have a conversation with The Legend Robert Rosie Rosenthal about his own experiences and conversations with the Piggyback Flight Pilot. I have said numerous times since that day how honored I am I to have Rosie Rosenthal's address and phone number in my parent's address book. And, the Rojohn family is grateful to have his son Dan as a friend.

Knowing what we know now, the Rojohn family wishes we would have attended the 2005 100th Bomb Group reunion with my mother in Pittsburgh, PA. We would have had the opportunity to talk with the veterans who witnessed the Piggyback Flight and had similar experiences as Captain Glenn H. Rojohn. We are thankful to their family members who have shared the stories we wanted to hear.

Connecting with the families of the Piggyback Flight, sharing the information about the legendary, historic Piggyback Flight has made our journey worthwhile. None of our fathers told us the story, we learned it together. We are so grateful for the memorabilia Captain Glenn H. Rojohn and his mother Selma left us so we can keep the story alive.

The Rojohn family knows our journey is not yet over. We are looking forward to the path we will continue to follow keeping the history alive.

We have been approached several times about a movie about the Piggyback Flight. The Rojohn and Piggyback Flight families hope and pray someday that will happen so everyone has an opportunity to learn about the Piggyback Flight Pilot's Journey, especially his 22nd Mission.

Thr Rojohn family thanks you for reading the Piggyback Flight Pilot's Journey. Please keep the stories and the legends of World War II alive.

CPSIA information can be obtained
at www.ICGtesting.com
Printed in the USA
LVHW070732130720
660481LV00003BA/7